Thankfully, Alina Gayeuski includes several laugh-out-loud anecdotes in her work. They leaven an otherwise sobering account of the church's continuing chilly climate, especially for women leaders. Her book makes clear that it was not enough to ordain women. The church needs to transform its culture into one that says equally to all people: this place is made for you.

—Dr. Karla Bohmbach, professor of religious studies at Susquehanna University, Selinsgrove, PA

With women more visible in church leadership, we often assume the issues that plague them are behind us. In *Beyond the Stained Glass Ceiling*, Pastor Gayeuski reminds us of the vital work still ahead and its transformative potential. With truth and hope, she illuminates these challenges and offers practical ways to build a more just church and world, beginning in our pulpits and pews. I highly recommend this book for church leaders and parishioners alike.

—Rev. Louise N. Johnson, executive for vision, Evangelical Lutheran Church in America

Endorsements for *Beyond the Stained Glass Ceiling*

If you thought the stained glass ceiling in the Protestant church was breached half a century ago with the ordination of women—or maybe when women were first consecrated as bishops – or surely, when a few women were named "head of communion"—if you have entertained such thoughts, Rev. Alina Gayeuski, in *Beyond the Stained Glass Ceiling,* urges you to think again. With devastating detail and evocative imagery (women clergy are like bicyclists in a city where all the cars are driven by men; ministry for women in a still-patriarchal church is like a river rafting trip where women are expected to portage around the dangerous patriarchal rapids – safer, perhaps, but still difficult, time-consuming and exhausting), Rev. Gayeuski describes a church not much more open to women's actual leadership than sixty years ago. Gayeuski, however, does not leave us depressed. With "the assurance of things hoped for, the conviction of things not seen," she describes a church that goes beyond representation to a theology of embodiment, including women's embodied experience, a church of truth-telling, of allies who become apostles, a church that sees the beauty of the divine in each and all of us, breaking the bonds of patriarchy and making way, at last, for a new beginning. May it be so.

— Rev. Dr. Sharon E. Watkins, General Minister and President (retired), Christian Church (Disciples of Christ) in the US and Canada

The challenges facing women in ministry are pervasive in the church, even among the mainline traditions where the ordination of women is accepted. These challenges are global. *Beyond the Stained Glass Ceiling: Women Clergy in a Still-Patriarchal Church* by Rev. Dr. Alina Gayeuski confronts this reality at a time when conversations about decolonizing the church must include confronting and eliminating patriarchal practices which continue to diminish the full inclusion and ministries of lay and ordained women.

— Rev. Dr. Karen Georgia Thompson, General Minister and President/Chief Executive Officer, United Church of Christ

Bold and courageously prophetic, *Beyond the Stained Glass Ceiling* is a timely, necessary, and urgent call to interrogate and deconstruct the decades of discrimination against female clergy. Gayeuski builds a strong and undeniable case for reforming the patriarchal structures that undergird and foment the sins of sexism in the church. Her visionary call to create a feminist church where all can flourish is compelling, hopeful, and inspiring.

—Rev. Dr. Leah D. Schade, associate professor of preaching and worship, Lexington Theological Seminary, author of *Preaching and Social Issues*

That which can't be named can't be healed. In this book, the bold Rev. Alina Gayeuski names the adaptive challenge of gender justice within the religious context. With courage and story, she explicitly describes the patriarchy that holds the church imprisoned, calling out the church she loves. And she calls in the same church to finally break the stained-glass ceiling and disrupt the system, so that the church can be, finally, a full expression of the God that calls each and every human beloved. Her message is finally hopeful, encouraging us to stay at it, until the church is freed and lives out the full expression of God incarnate.

—Mary Kay DuChene, co-director of LeaderWise and co-author of *A Path to Belonging: Overcoming Clergy Loneliness*

In *Beyond the Stained Glass Ceiling*, Rev. Dr. Alina Gayeuski invites us into the start of a difficult and essential conversation for the church: Why are female clergy still being excluded, blocked, condescended to, and oppressed in their leadership roles in the church? Gayeuski's clear and compelling voice also invites us into a future church, a feminist church, where all can flourish. Sharp critique joins creative vision in this eye-opening and hope-inspiring little book.

—Dr. Jon Pahl PhD, Peter Paul and Elizabeth Hagan Professor of the History of Christianity, United Lutheran Seminary, Gettysburg/Philadelphia, and author of *Fethullah Gulen: A Life of Hizmet, Why a Muslim Scholar in Pennsylvania Matters to the World*

This book is an urgent summons to all who envision a church where women can thrive without sacrificing the fullness of who we are. Gayeuski calls us to do more than put incremental cracks in the stained-glass ceiling. She hands us a hammer with which to smash the patriarchy so thoroughly that new systems can emerge to welcome the courageous witness of those who move through the world in women's bodies.

—Rev. Christa M. Compton, PhD, bishop of the New Jersey Synod of the ELCA

Beyond the Stained Glass Ceiling offers information, education, and inspiration aimed at transforming individuals, congregations, and institutions. Through personal stories and examples of discrimination, the book urges the church to reform its teachings on what it means to be a Beloved child of God serving in ordained ministry and beyond, supported by Romans 8:28. This book serves as a practical tool for Bible studies, call committees, and seminaries.

—Rev. Dr. Patricia Davenport, former bishop, Southeastern Pennsylvania Synod, ELCA

Written skillfully and rooted in experience as well as research, this book is a much-needed exploration of the issues women clergy encounter within the patriarchal structures of the church. Gayeuski proposes feminist pathways for overcoming them and for transforming the ecclesial culture into one of flourishing for women ministers.

—Dr. Natalia Marandiuc, associate professor of systematic theology and director of Women, Gender, and Sexuality Program, United Lutheran Seminary

Why are women leaving both pulpits and pews behind? Alina Gayeuski has a timely answer: they are finished conforming to the futile patriarchal frameworks built into our sanctuaries. She makes her case, grounded in the history of feminism, solid research, classic fairytales, playground games, and heartbreaking accounts from present-day women clergy. Alina Gayeuski is a prophet for our times, inviting the reader to settle for nothing less than liberation.

—emilie boggis, LeaderWise staff consultant, spiritual director, reflective pastoral supervisor and ordained minister

Once and a while you read something that sparks your imagination to what might be if we work together to create change. *Beyond the Stained Glass Ceiling* does just that. The patriarchy is strong in the world and in the church, but Alina Gayeuski's book helps us to see past that so that we can work together to break down the barriers to women serving fully and powerfully in the church today.

—Rev. Dr. Karyn L Wiseman, the Stuempfle-Folkemer Professor of Homiletics, United Lutheran Seminary, Gettysburg + Philadelphia, author of *Queering the Pulpit: A Sexegetical Approach to Preaching an Inclusive Word*

Beyond the Stained Glass Ceiling addresses the important topic of women clergy and oppressive anti-feminist church systems. Gayeuski delves into the intricacies of the deep-rooted patriarchy in the church, and ways to dismantle these patriarchal systems. Interviews and personal stories are masterfully woven together with intensive research, and because of this book, the reader will have a better understanding of women clergy and patriarchy, as well as hope for a different future within the church.

—Rev. Dr. Becca Ehrlich, author of *Christian Minimalism: Simple Steps for Abundant Living,* executive director of New Breath Spirituality Center and Spiritual Director (Albany and Saratoga Springs, NY)

This book is a must-read for anyone who cares deeply about the church and the call to live in right and just relationship with one another. Gayeuski bears witness to the lived realities that the vast majority of women clergy continue to experience sexism in their callings. It insightfully wrestles with how women's ordination did not change the patriarchal bedrock of the church, and envisions what a feminist church might look like instead. Whether you're a clergywoman yourself or more broadly someone who holds hope for a church that embodies liberation, this book is for you.

—Crystal L. Hall, PhD, coach for women in ministry

WOMEN CLERGY IN A
STILL-PATRIARCHAL CHURCH

BEYOND THE *Stained Glass* CEILING

ALINA GAYEUSKI

Copyright © 2026 Alina Gayeuski. Printed by Chalice Press. All rights reserved.

All rights reserved. For permission to reuse content, please contact Copyright Clearance Center, 222 Rosewood Drive, Danvers, MA 01923, (978) 750-8400, www.copyright.com.

Bible quotations, unless otherwise noted, are from the *New Revised Standard Version Bible,* copyright 1989, Division of Christian Education of the National Council of the Churches of Christ in the United States of America. Used by permission. All rights reserved.

Print: 9780827203532

EPUB: 9780827203549

EPDF: 9780827203556

ChalicePress.com

Contents

Note to the Reader

This book contains the stories of many women clergy who have boldly and courageously shared their experiences of sexism within the church. To protect their identity, the stories have been anonymized and each story assigned a random pseudonym. If a story is presented with a person's real identity, it is detailed in the citation. These stories represent the diversity of experiences that women clergy face every day. Some are stories of assault or harassment. Please read with care.

Introduction

Struggles to end patriarchy are divinely ordained.
—bell hooks[1]

When I told my mom I wanted to go to seminary, she cried.

Hers were not tears of joy, but rather ones filled with fear. My mom knew all too well what it would mean for me to become a pastor, particularly as a young woman. Because of that, I had strategized when and where to tell her, knowing that she might not be excited immediately. I figured telling her in the middle of the day in her office would be the best way to limit her reaction—especially considering where she worked.

My mom started a job at my home church when I was eight. She worked as the coordinator of senior services, a position I often describe as being the youth director for senior citizens. Our congregation's membership of more than three thousand people meant that my mom was always busy working with those over sixty-five in the congregation—helping them navigate everything from moving to a retirement community to Medicare to grocery shopping to loss and grief. Because of her job, I was lucky to have countless bonus grandparents who loved seeing me when I would tag along with my mom on days off from school.

But this job also meant that my mom had a front-row seat to how the female pastors of my congregation were treated. Because the staff was comprised of multiple clergy, she saw that treatment in contrast to the way the male pastors were treated. She saw the day-to-day encounters that the women clergy had to navigate. She knew of the time a female pastor was asked not to officiate a wedding because she would "ruin the photos." She heard the times people asked the women clergy, "Is the pastor in?" She had witnessed the ways that people intentionally sought to undermine the authority of the clergywomen by withholding or changing important information.

[1] bell hooks, *Feminism is for Everybody: Passionate Politics* (South End Press, 2000), 107.

She knew what these women experienced and had seen their tears as well.

Unfortunately, my mother knew more than anyone what it would mean for me to be a pastor and to be treated as less than I deserve. She had witnessed the painful realities of these women pastors whom she worked alongside. She knew and she mourned, realizing what she had witnessed would be true for her daughter. So she cried.

I wish my mom's fears had been unfounded. I wish that this was one of those exceedingly rare times when my mother was wrong. But over the last decade-plus of my ministry, I have watched my mother's fears come true for me and my female colleagues.

Yet, also like my mother, I am not one to let injustices have the final say on our world nor let them compromise what the church should be about in this world. My mother's deep faith and strong commitment to the church are part of my story just as much as anything else is. She instilled in me a love for living as part of a community of faith and recognized my call to ministry. She did not let her fears try to dissuade me, even if they caused her grief.

But there must be more than just pushing down fears and hoping for the best. Those of us who care about the church have come to a point where we need to name the hold that sexism has continued to have on the institution despite more than half a century of the right to ordination for women in mainline denominations. We need to build a future shaped by God's call for equity and justice, one in which the next generation of women clergy will be celebrated and their mothers' fears will be calmed. Only then can we truly move forward in a way that will liberate all people.

More Than a Mother's Intuition

The experiences my mother witnessed were not outliers. The statistics support every fear my mom had for the reality my female colleagues and I continue to live now. To begin with, women are still not a notable part of the demographic of religious leaders in the United States. Less than 10 percent of Americans who regularly attend worship do so at a church in which a woman is the primary leader. This is despite the fact that more than half of religiously affiliated Americans attend churches of denominations in which women's ordination is permitted, as well as that most of these denominations have permitted women's ordination for decades.[2]

Why are women clergy still so underrepresented within the leadership of American congregations? Regardless of the permission to become ordained, women have never received full support from the church. Rather than the church adjusting to welcome and embrace the leadership of women, the patriarchal structures upon which the church has been based for centuries remain steadfast. As such, the burden remains on women clergy as they are forced to navigate or find ways to survive these structures. This book seeks to name the ways clergywomen have been taught to survive the patriarchal structures of the church and what happens when they are unsuccessful. But this book is also about what it would mean to create a feminist church where all can thrive.

Perhaps a helpful illustration is an analogy I once heard: Being a woman is like being a cyclist in a city where all the cars are driven by men. Even if the roads are meant to be used for both bicycles and motor vehicles, that is obviously not the way it works. There is an extreme level of mental and physical energy needed to navigate around vehicles that are larger and faster. The potential for serious injury is a constant companion. Some drivers believe the cyclists have no business even being in a small and precarious designated bike lane in the first place and may even want to force them off the road. And if the worst outcome occurs and the cyclist is hurt, it will likely be counted as their fault. After all, how could they expect safety in this environment?

Sadly, this problem is just as true for the church, if not more so. After all, the church tends to lag behind society in terms of how best to be with and for others. Throughout my ministry I have experienced and witnessed this sexism. For me, that is as a pastor of the Evangelical Lutheran Church in America (ELCA) the denomination in which I was raised and ordained. But this truth pervades throughout mainline Protestantism in the United States. It is something I continue to witness among my colleagues in Young Clergy Women

[2] Benjamin R. Knoll and Cammie Jo Bolin, *She Preached the Word: Women's Ordination in Modern America* (Oxford University Press, 2018), 32.

International—a worldwide professional organization for women clergy under forty. Repeatedly, women in this group tell stories of the ways they have been taught to work around the patriarchy and, if they fail, choose between the church and themselves.

My clergy sisters and I have come to know a painful truth: patriarchy has lied to us. We have been convinced by the structures built by patriarchal ideology that achievement would liberate us from the oppressions placed upon us. Achieving the right to pursue ordination seemed like overcoming the greatest barrier for women in the church. That was our stained glass ceiling to break. But once that threshold was passed, the oppressions morphed into something new.

As someone born after the right to ordination was granted to women in my denomination, I have never known a time when it was not possible. I have also never known a time when it was fully embraced and celebrated. Women have been kept from key leadership roles, told they were undeserving of the places they have been called, and systematically punished for their bodies, sexuality, and feminine experiences. The right to ordination has not provided protection from any of these truths.

Worse still is the way women clergy have been taught by the same oppressive systems to accept and navigate this reality. Clergywomen have been taught and encouraged to change the way they dress, speak, and lead—often contrary to the way they would do so naturally or intuitively and in a way that is completely unnecessary for the job. The assumption behind this is that the church will not change and the best hope is to navigate around and survive. This is the greatest obstacle to women's leadership. The church that allowed for women's ordination never changed in structure to embrace women's ordination. Until that happens, there will be no liberative leadership for women in the church and women leaders will continue to leave their roles to the detriment of the whole church.

Why Now?

In 2020 my denomination celebrated three milestone ordination anniversaries: the fiftieth anniversary of the ordination of (white) women, the fortieth anniversary of the ordination of women of color, and the tenth anniversary of the ordination of openly queer clergy. As is often the case with these types of marks in history, there is an intentional opportunity for reflection. In preparation for this historic moment, the 2019 ELCA Churchwide Assembly—a triennial gathering of representatives from across the denomination—included a special worship service to celebrate the anniversary of the ordination of women. I watched this celebration worship, and as the procession of women clergy—a procession taking more than five minutes—ranging in age from their mid-twenties to 104, entered the worship space, I was overcome with emotion. These women, all they had accomplished, all they had been through, and all they represented brought hope and joy.

Yet sometimes hope and joy can be fleeting. Many of those women would return to churches and communities where the fullness of their identity would not be celebrated or valued or where they would continue to encounter sexism that limited their ability to lead. The painful truth of the experiences of clergywomen plays out every day, in more ways than can ever be counted or known. I came to hold the tension of that celebration worship alongside the daily realities I knew women clergy were experiencing.

And the statistics proved it. My denomination did a study at the forty-fifth anniversary and again at the fiftieth anniversary to examine the experiences of women clergy.[3] In those five short years, the percentage of women who experienced gender-based discrimination increased in every category studied: in seminary, during internship, in the congregation/ministry setting, with other ELCA clergy, during the call process, with ecumenical colleagues, and by synod/churchwide staff. In the fiftieth anniversary study, 65 percent of women clergy reported experiencing gender-based discrimination in at least one of these areas.

As I prepared to write this book, I shared the topic with several groups—many of them clergy groups. The reactions varied among people. Some were shocked to find out that these experiences

[3] "50th Anniversary Ordination of Women Survey Report," Evangelical Lutheran Church in America, August 2021, updated March 2022, https://resources.elca.org/gender-justice-and-womens-empowerment/50th-anniversary-ordination-of-women-survey-report-2/.

were still this prevalent for women clergy; others simply nodded in understanding. But it was often the older clergywomen who responded in ways that would arguably make this work seem unnecessary. They said things like: "You could have written this when I was in seminary thirty years ago," or "These are the things I've experienced my whole career; it isn't going to change." It is heartbreaking to hear such comments, especially knowing the lifetime of oppression these foremothers have experienced within and from the church. But their comments represent the success of the patriarchy. One of the most common tools of these oppressive structures is to convince women that this is the way things are and will always be. This maintains the status quo and enables patriarchy to thrive. It also creates a culture that teaches women to navigate these structures without hope of a better way.

Sexism has become so commonplace that we are either ignorant to see it or hopeless to think it will ever change. These older clergywomen embody just that—the way they have been convinced that these experiences are not important enough or do not represent sexism. Or those who know the truth are often exhausted from decades of fighting for their full inclusion without much change. After all, if women can be ordained and, at least in theory, take on the same leadership as men in the church, what else could be needed?

The first and perhaps most important task we must take on is naming that sexism is very real and still very much exists. Women daily live with everything from microaggressions to attacks of sexual violence. Together we will name this real and painful truth: sexism is alive and well in the church. This needs to continue to be publicly acknowledged in the church until the belief that we are past such oppressive behaviors is dislodged. This is a significant hurdle to this work and any other work that attempts to liberate people from our human-made oppressions.

I have experienced sexism personally and heard many stories from others. After over a decade in ordained ministry, I see the patterns emerging from the stories my colleagues share and from the experiences of those who have forged the path before us. I understand that my ancestors in this battle for gender equality are tired. The work of feminists who have gone before us is significant, and the gains they made are vital to our collective future. At the same time patriarchy worked just as hard to convince us that feminist gains were enough and we should move on or even give up. But if we do so, patriarchy strengthens its grasp, further restricting the hope of liberation.

Part of considering why now is the time for this work must address why the focus of this book is on women clergy. After all, women in all sectors of life continue to experience deep and inhibiting obstacles to achieving the fullness of what they are called to be and do in this world because of patriarchal structures. In fact, in sharing my work with women in the church who are not clergy, I have been told over and over again how much these stories resonate with their own experiences. But that is exactly the reason women clergy are our starting point. I believe the way we treat women in the pulpit directly impacts the way we think about women in the pews. The research proves it. This work is for our collective liberation.

This is especially important as our world feels as though it is careening toward a time when women's autonomy and agency are under constant attack. Many rights or privileges that were assumed to be guaranteed protections have been removed and the very lives of women are at risk. With the overturning of *Roe v. Wade* in 2022, we saw a harbinger of what else might become true for women.

We cannot be content to sit by and allow these systems to continue. I discovered this lesson early on in my life when I learned that systems that are meant to keep rolling would never stop. When I was three years old my parents took me on my first trip to the beach for a week of vacation. Within the first few minutes of being at the shoreline, a wave crashed in front of me and knocked me down, filling my eyes, nose, and mouth with salt water. Once my parents dried me off, bundled me in a towel, and consoled me back on our blanket, I declared that I would not be going back into the water until the waves stopped.

Like the waves of the ocean, systems of oppression are built to continue rolling—often knocking over anyone in their way. The repetition of the waves shows that as much as things change, they remain the same. The same can be said for the ways patriarchy continues to turn on the shores of women's lives. I feel called to speak and act now. My hope is, even if in just a small way, this work might be an act of resistance.

Who Is This For?

This book is for everyone who takes the call to live out God's justice in this world seriously. While this book focuses on the stories and experiences of clergywomen, it does so as a metric. These stories tell us something about what the church is like and how that impacts the ability for all people to participate fully in the community we are building together because of the gospel and for the sake of the world.

By bringing attention to the experiences of my women clergy colleagues and my own ministry, I hope to show that there is still much work to be done to move past the patriarchy that continues to have a hold on the church (and the whole world for that matter). Yet, in the church, we are called to a different way of being and a different way of living. We are called to work against the powers of this world that would keep us from God and the ways of God's love. The church is called to be a model of God's liberation in a world that tries to bind us all.

My hope is that this book will move us to new places. That might look like congregation leadership teams discussing changes to personnel policies that are more equitable and just. Or it might look like denominational staff considering how they raise up leaders who have often been passed over for positions. Or it might look like a call committee asking why they have never had a woman pastor serve their congregation.

But most of all, I hope that it looks like the start of many honest conversations about what God is calling the church to and how God is calling all of us to be together in this world. We need to fully recognize that we have not overcome sexism or any other oppressive power. These forces will always find a way to change and adapt to hold power over others. But we can choose to refuse complicity and ignorance and instead move toward justice and wholeness for all of God's people.

As such, this book is for everyone who cares deeply about the church and the way that we are called to be in relationship with and for each other. These issues are beyond any one group of people, any one gender identity, or any one vocation. This issue is about the way we are called into community and entrusted with building up the body of Christ in this world. This book invites you to think about the problems women clergy face, what they mean for the whole church, and the way that we all might be called into the future God hopes for all people.

Defining Language

Language can always liberate and limit us—and sometimes do both simultaneously. How we choose what we say and mean what we say is a constantly changing reality. Nevertheless, there are things we need to define, even if they fall short of representing that which might be beyond words. Many additional topics and issues will be defined in the pages ahead; however, these initial definitions will help us as we begin.

For the purpose of this book, "women" will mean those who have been socialized as women—that is, those who, typically because of the sex assigned to them at birth, have been treated in particular ways representing a narrative connected to gender identity and expression. This does not mean this is the best way to engage in the ways of understanding sex and gender, but rather a recognition of the way our society functions.

There are additional obstacles and oppressions for those who experience marginalization in addition to sex and/or gender. We must recognize that all of the challenges placed in front of women clergy to fully embody the roles they have been called to are made more difficult for those simultaneously experiencing racism, xenophobia, homophobia, transphobia, and other -isms and phobias. These oppressions continue to disproportionately impact women and make their lives that much harder.

The voices and stories shared throughout this book represent a full diversity of women from various backgrounds and will recognize many obstacles faced by those representing other marginalized identities. Other oppressive forces work best when paired with patriarchy. In all ways, sexism seeks to hold power over others and will align itself with any other force that desires the same. Since this book focuses primarily on the issue of gender bias, the full impact of these intersecting oppressions will not be completely represented.

There is also an important distinction to be made between sex and gender identity. While sex refers to the designation made at birth, labeling someone as "female" or "male" based on reproductive organs, gender is a socially constructed designation. With full recognition that being assigned female at birth does not have a direct correlation with being socialized as a woman, throughout this book "female" and "woman" will often be used interchangeably for a variety of language and not meant to be a conflation of terms. The use of "man" set in opposition to "woman" is not to indicate a gender binary—the idea that there are only two genders—but rather is an indication of the historic societal construction of patriarchal structures along with the benefiting or oppressed identities.

"Clergy" will mean those who have been set apart in their particular tradition for official leadership, typically through ordination or consecration. For many denominations this looks like people serving as pastors, priests, deacons, or ministers. Issues related to patriarchy in traditions in which women's ordination or official leadership is not allowed or supported, such as the Roman Catholic Church, are beyond what is possible in these pages. Yet this book is rooted in the hope that all women will be liberated from any patriarchal structures that limit them to live into the fullness of who God has created them to be and that those denominations and expressions of the church will also seek justice in these matters.

Likewise, references to "the church" in these pages will almost always reflect experiences within mainline Protestantism in the United States. This designation reflects denominations that have permitted the ordination of women since at least the 1970s. This includes my own experience within the ELCA and that of my clergywomen colleagues in Young Clergy Women International who also serve in the largest Protestant denominations within the country, such as the United Methodist Church, the Presbyterian Church (USA), the United Church of Christ, and the Episcopal Church.

In order to discuss these realities of patriarchy, we first need to define it. Simply put, this is the belief that men are superior to women. When this belief becomes systematized and controls everything from decisions to policies, it becomes a source of oppression. In the church, this is the root of the belief that women should not or cannot be clergy or that they will be less skilled than men at the work of ministry. Patriarchy centers the experiences of men* (*white, straight, educated, middle- to upper-class men) and defines everything using that as the norm. The experiences of women are left out of consideration—and, as a result, so are women.

We also must define feminism. This word is often misunderstood as having a limited definition of advancing the place or experience of women in this world. But it is much more. Feminism is the way in which we must actively acknowledge and challenge the impacts that patriarchy has on everyone. This oppression, like all oppressions, impacts the ability for all people to fully live as God intended for us. Feminism is a commitment to equity and justice, far beyond sex and gender. Yet, because of the long history of oppressing women, to enact feminism is to celebrate and champion women. This is a commitment the church must take up.

Giving Voice

This book will be rooted in the feminist work that it seeks to do. The lived experiences of women will be essential to addressing and understanding these issues. This book will center the voices of women clergy who live this reality of the church. In so doing, it will root our understanding of this problem and the impacts in the experience of these women clergy. My research includes correspondence and interviews with women clergy. These women have been told that who they are is incompatible with what the church wants from its clergy. They have been encouraged to work around the patriarchal structures of the church and endured consequences on their leadership as a result of the workarounds to avoid the realities of patriarchy. They have been told to change themselves to be tolerable or, at best, acceptable.

The clergywomen who shared their stories and experiences for this book are members and friends of Young Clergy Women International. This organization started over two decades ago when a group of clergywomen started gathering each summer to share the joys and challenges of being a young woman in professional ministry. Over time this organization has grown to more than 2,500 members and alumnae worldwide. I am privileged to be part of this organization where I also served on the board and as a past chair of the board. But more so, I am grateful for this community of young clergywomen who champion and support each other, embodying the church we wish to know. The voices of the women in this book are a gift to the whole church.

My own stories and experiences will also be woven into these pages. As such, it is necessary to name my personal location in the world. I am a white, straight, cisgender—meaning my gender identity matches the sex I was assigned at birth—woman who is married to a man who also serves as a pastor in my denomination. I have had the privilege of access to education, including seminary, which supported my own path to ordination. I serve in the ELCA as the lead pastor and part of an all-female clergy team at a midsized congregation in the suburbs of Philadelphia.

This book will help to amplify the voices of women in the church who are also starting to name these issues and dream of a more egalitarian future. While these pages can only provide a limited glimpse into this work, I am grateful for the ability to build on the work of others in looking at what might be possible. There will also be illustrations and examples pulled from contemporary sources and popular culture. I believe the church is not a city on a hill, but rather part of the world that continues to shape and define the way it looks and operates. To consider this work absent from the influences of the secular would be detrimental to a full understanding of how we live with all of these parts of our world.

Last, but perhaps most essential, this book will stand on the shoulders of feminists who have gone ahead and set the path for so much of this work to be possible today. These pages will echo their voices and the revelations about patriarchy and feminism they brought to light. These women who have written and taught and preached have informed and inspired me. Because of these individuals—some famous and others only known to those they inspire—many others are able to have their work continue the legacy of women who have sought a seat at the table—and, even more importantly, a place to preside at the table. I am grateful for their witness and the gift they offer the church.

The Journey Forward

The pages ahead will dive deeply into these issues, considering this problem women clergy encounter from all angles. That is because, like so many things, this is a dynamic issue, caught up in history and theology and the very lives of the women who are called to preach and teach in the church.

For too long we have relied on old structures of "doing" church that have limited the full participation of all people, especially women. This book will explore the particular ways women clergy have been encouraged to work around the existing patriarchal structures in order to survive them—and, worse, what happens when they fail to navigate these obstacles and the ways they are treated.

But this book will also be about what the future can hold.

Despite the painful depths and pervasiveness of this problem in the church, the overwhelming basis of this book is hope. There are already signs within our world that there is still a worthwhile fight against these patriarchal structures. The final part of this book will be future-oriented, with tangible descriptions of what a feminist church will look like for the full inclusion and celebration of all of God's people, especially the generations of clergywomen to come. This work has inspired hope in me. My prayer is that it will help you dream about the future of the church and inspire hope anew for you too.

Chapter 1

From Votes to Vestments

Society does well at naming the symptoms that the illness of patriarchy produces in this world. Quick internet searches reveal that women, on average, earn 83 percent of what their male counterparts earn, that less than 30 percent of the U.S. Congress is female, and that CEOs who happen to be women make up barely 10 percent of the leadership of Fortune 500 companies. Throughout the history of the United States, there have been only fifty-three female governors as of 2026, only three have been women of color, and only two have been openly queer women.[1,2,3,4,5] The gravity of these facts and figures might suggest there would be a greater impetus to seek out the cause of these inequities. But patriarchal structures are more stable when the source of the problem remains unnamed or unspoken, making them harder to identify and more challenging for women to navigate. This creates the real issue—keeping the burden of these structures on women.

[1] theSkimm Staff, "The State of Women," *theSkimm*, March 9, 2023, https://www.theskimm.com/stateofwomen/harris-poll-data-2023.

[2] Amy Diehl, Leanne M. Dzubinski, and Amber L. Stephenson, "New Research Reveals the 30 Critiques Holding Women Back from Leadership that Most Men Will Never Hear," *Fast Company*, May 2, 2023, https://www.fastcompany.com/90889985/new-research-reveals-critiques-holding-women-back-from-leadership-that-most-men-will-never-hear.

[3] "History of Women Governors," Center for American Women and Politics, Eagleton Institute of Politics, Rutgers University-New Brunswick, 2025, https://cawp.rutgers.edu/facts/levels-office/statewide-elective-executive/history-women-governors.

[4] Caitlin O'Kane, "Maura Healey and Tina Kotek Make History, Winning Elections to Be First Openly Lesbian U.S. Governors," *CBS News*, November 8, 2022, https://www.cbsnews.com/news/maura-healey-massachusetts-tina-kotek-oregon-elected-governor-first-openly-lesbian-history/.

[5] Lisa Intrabartola, "What Mikie Sherrill and Abigail Spanberger's Gubernatorial Wins Mean for Women in Politics," Rutgers, November 5, 2025, https://www.rutgers.edu/news/what-mikie-sherrill-and-abigail-spanbergers-gubernatorial-wins-mean-women-politics.

One illustration of this is the "motherhood penalty/fatherhood premium" found in the workplace. Often advice is given to men interviewing for a job that they should mention their family, as it presents them as more stable and reliable. Women are advised the opposite—to avoid any mention of a family at an interview. The belief is that women who are preoccupied with children and a spouse are less committed and less dependable. Even though it is illegal to hire (or not hire) for these reasons, the bias against women dominates, even subconsciously—and it is up to women to protect themselves from these experiences by cautiously sharing their lives while interviewing. This bias then extends into salary realities once individuals have the job. Women lose earnings when they become a mother; men gain additional earnings when they become a father[6]—further exacerbating an already inequitable pay gap between the genders.

This issue has manifested itself in ways that impact women in all spheres of life. Women need to navigate around the obstacles and barriers that patriarchy has built, hindering their full potential. For women clergy, the church has been no different. Like all parts of our society that have been built by and for men, the church forces women to compromise in order to survive. Women clergy bear the most significant burden in this as they have attempted to enter the leadership ranks—spaces that for nearly two millennia were formally held almost exclusively by men.

So how did we get here? That is the real question we must grapple with before we can consider what might be possible for a future free from these oppressions. To better understand where we are, we have to look at what has brought us to this moment. After all, patriarchy has a long and troubled history of oppression. The way that women clergy experience it in today's church is only a glimpse at the diligent efforts of sexism to build up these structures of hindrance and exclusion.

Even more so, this will be a chance to look at how we have arrived at this current point in the life of the church. Like so many things,

[6] Sari Pekkala Kerr, "The Motherhood Penalty and the Fatherhood Premium: The Gender Wage Gap Across the Family Life Cycle," Wellesley Centers for Women, https://www.wcwonline.org/Research-Action-Annual-Report-2022/the-motherhood-penalty-and-the-fatherhood-premium-the-gender-wage-gap-across-the-family-life-cycle.

the only way to know what is happening now is to understand how we ended up here in the first place.

Waves of Feminism

The history of feminism in the United States is both complicated and complicating. It simultaneously holds points of celebration and times of confession. It is our responsibility to name that and use this truth as the basis of our work for the future.

As we look through each of the waves of feminist history in the pages ahead, there will be points of significant success as well as many serious shortcomings. It is important to name as we move through this history that much of our narrative for the successes of feminism is often only about "white feminism"—that is, a feminism that has prioritized and privileged the experiences of white women.

This is not to say that advances made for any women as a result of feminist movements in history are not important and revolutionary in their own right. Yet, if we do not hold this tension, we risk continuing to uphold successes that were limited and erase errors that had grave consequences. Worse yet, we continue cycles of oppression that leave out women who are not white, straight, married, educated, or embodied in any other point of privilege in society. Considering each wave of feminism in a way that identifies both the advances some women made and the costs to other women is necessary to break this cycle and truly liberate all women.

Due to the span of time and the unending impacts of each part of this history, this section will provide a relatively brief review. Yet this review of significant events and themes will help us to better understand our current reality. These issues have played out in paralleling ways in the church, and those will be highlighted as well.

Like all history, there are names and dates and movements that we must explore. Without knowing them, we cannot come to fully know ourselves and the future we are building.

First Wave

The women in long, white dresses with their "Votes for Women" sashes are probably the most well-known image of the first wave of feminism. These women of the late nineteenth and early twentieth centuries who worked to secure the right for women to vote are iconic in their representation of this movement. Known as suffragettes, they became associated with their public activism and organization to protest the lack of voting rights for women.

Initially their activism also included advocating for the abolition of slavery. Yet, despite the frequent alignment of suffragettes with the abolitionist movement, they were also greatly opposed to the passing of the Fifteenth Amendment—which provided Black men the right to vote before white women. There seemed to be a disconnect between their belief that Black persons living under the oppression of slavery should be free and any belief that they should have the same rights in the country as their white counterparts—or, at the very least, not before white women. (It would take another fifty years after the passing of the Fifteenth Amendment until the passing of the Nineteenth Amendment, which would grant all women the right to vote. However, additional voting laws would continue to limit the access of Black women to the polls for years to come.) Elizabeth Cady Stanton most notoriously embodied these parts of this time in history; she publicly championed the right of white women to vote and criticized the right of Black men to vote.

The suffragettes believe that adding the voices of white women to the election process would "civilize" society. After all, many white women fully recognized the role they played in sustaining societal structures by running households, caring for children, and managing economics. Without being able to vote, their logic followed, they were unable to lend their expertise in these areas to the further betterment of society. The counter-narrative, even if unspoken, was that Black women were not seen as having the same ability to add to the positive reform of society. But it was intentional.

Nonetheless, we continue to celebrate, within our societal narrative, the work of the suffragettes to further the rights of women. We do this at the expense of Black women—and many others—who the suffragettes were willing and able to leave out of their search for justice. We must reckon with the historical significance of the right to vote being afforded to white women and of the many who were left out of such rights.

Second Wave

It was my junior year of college when I first picked up Betty Friedan's groundbreaking work, *The Feminine Mystique,* which was required reading for one of my women's studies classes. Many scholars consider this publication to be the spark that ignited the start of second-wave feminism. In her book, Friedan writes about "the problem that has no name"—that is, the malaise felt by women who had achieved the life that society had prescribed for them.[7] These homemaking women of the 1950s had abandoned any aspirations that did not include marriage, motherhood, and managing the household while their husbands worked in the 9-to-5 corporate world. Women suffered, and patriarchy thrived. Friedan's work threatened the power of this belief by saying what millions of women were feeling.

Decades later, Hollywood would put this same issue on the big screen with the production of *Mona Lisa Smile* featuring Julia Roberts. As a professor in an all-girls college, Roberts' character became disenchanted by the lack of ambition that the girls she taught exhibited—with many making it clear they were only there to get their "MRS" degree (that is, the purpose of their education was purely match-making in nature—helping them become a "Mrs.").

Whether you look at Friedan's initial description of this issue or Roberts' theatrical embodiment, there was a truth to this problem and the way it was impacting women. Indeed, these limitations were creating an un-survivable reality for women. But Friedan's work was shortsighted and has been rightly criticized by other feminist theorists for centering the experiences of white women—and even more specifically middle-class, straight, married, white women—and considering them to be universal realities. She ignored the privilege that this location in the world afforded her and others suffering in this particular way. In the words of bell hooks, when Friedan wrote of the "problem that has no name," "she ignored the existence of all non-white women and poor white women."[8]

---

[7] Betty Friedan, *The Feminine Mystique* (New York: W.W. Norton & Company, 1963).

[8] bell hooks, *Feminist Theory: From Margin to Center* (Boston: South End Press, 1984), 2.

While it is true that the lives of many women were confined to the expectations of society, they also embodied a privilege of which they were possibly unaware but definitely perpetuated. The ability of white women to fill this role of homemaker typically meant that they were educated, married, and belonged to a certain economic demographic in this country. This expectation limited what they might have been able to accomplish otherwise. However, the same would not be true for women who could not benefit from those same privileges. The struggle for justice and a place in this world is not the same for all women. Without the recognition of the multiple oppressions that weigh heavily on others, the progress of anyone but white women was nearly impossible.

A response to this truth was the creation of "womanism," a concept credited to the work of Alice Walker, who first coined the term and defined it. For Walker, womanism meant the ability to consider the struggle non-white women experienced with the further oppressions due to racism. As she famously equated: "Womanism is to feminism as purple is to lavender"[9]—meaning that womanism embodied a broader, more holistic understanding of sexism and accompanying oppressions. Because of theorists like Walker, people were forced to recognize the intersecting identities of women and the additional obstacles society placed in the way of their liberation from sexism.

Despite shortcomings, Friedan's work rang a bell that could not be unrung. It signaled to many women that they were not alone in these feelings and experiences and started a movement. Women started entering and making advancements in realms that had previously been reserved for men, albeit, with significant privileging of white women into these roles that had previously been reserved for white men.

In paralleling experiences, this was also the dawning of feminist theology that would critique the way patriarchy was embedded and enabled by the church. Theologians like Mary Daly, with her double-headed axe and her infamous equation that "if God is male, then

---

[9] Alice Walker, *In Search of Our Mothers' Gardens,* (New York City: Open Road Media, 1983), xii.

male is God,"[10] began to unsettle the hold that sexism had over the hierarchy of the church. Like Friedan, Daly and her contemporaries challenged the hold that patriarchy had on the church, and these issues could no longer be ignored. Daly's work, in particular, because of her directness, began to disrupt the two millennia-long hold that patriarchy had on the church. Unsurprisingly, Daly was met with resistance and risked dismissal from her tenured position at Boston College following the publication of her book *The Church and the Second Sex.* The discomfort of pulling back the veil of patriarchy in the church was almost too much for the system to bear, and Daly came close to experiencing retaliatory consequences from men who wanted to maintain their own positions of power.

But Daly was unrelenting and held firm to her position that removing the old, patriarchal structures of the church would give way to new feminist experience. She saw the unfolding of this potential outside the church, and her writings sparked movement for the benefit of women inside the church. The same reckoning that was occurring in the secular spaces of society was beginning to unfold in the spiritual. Like Friedan's, Daly's work was limited to her white experience. The church privileged the advancement of white women over Black women.

As a result of this influence of the women's movement on religion, during this time the greatest visible advancements for the roles of women in the church were gained. Mainline Protestant denominations began permitting the ordination and leadership of women in all levels of the church. My own denomination's predecessor bodies, the Lutheran Church in America and the American Lutheran Church, both voted in 1970 to allow for the ordination of women, and that November Rev. Elizabeth Platz became the first female Lutheran pastor ordained in the United States. More women began entering seminaries and divinity schools and started holding leadership in local congregations and denominational judicatories. It would take another decade before a Lutheran denomination in the United States would celebrate the ordination of a woman of color when Rev. Erlean Miller was ordained.

[10] Mary Daly, *Beyond God the Father: Toward a Philosophy of Women's Liberation* (Boston: Beacon Press, 1973), 19.

During this same time many other mainline denominations joined with the same right for women's ordination: the Presbyterian Church (USA) and the Methodist Church in 1956[11,12]; the Episcopal Church in 1976 (although eleven women were ordained in Philadelphia two years prior into the official policy)[13]; the Reformed Church in America granted partial privileges in 1972 and full ordination rights in 1979[14]; and the Moravian Church in North America gave the right to ordination in 1970 but did not ordain the first woman until 1975.[15]

All of these accomplishments, despite being revolutionary and essential, were limited. As women continued entering the public spheres at an increased rate, society had to reckon with what allowances or adjustments would be made. Because of this reality, women who were granted these rights were never granted any additional considerations. Other societal or cultural accommodations would not be made, such as considerations around child care, home responsibilities, and other things that remain de facto responsibilities for women. In fact, women would just be added to the pre-existing structures and would have to hope for the best. When the successes were unsustainable, the women who seemed to overreach would be the only ones to blame.

This is a seductive path for patriarchy. It means that the least amount of power is sacrificed and with less effort the equilibrium can be reattained. There was little that would change; and, as such, this progress would be short-lived.

---

[11] Presbyterian News Services, "PC(USA) Celebrates 60 Years of Women Clergy," PC(USA), May 24, 2016, https://pcusa.org/news-storytelling/news/2016/5/24/pcusa-celebrates-60-years-women-clergy.

[12] Tom McInally, "Commentary: Why Do United Methodists Ordain Women When the Bible Specifically Prohibits It?" The United Methodist Church, https://www.umc.org/en/content/commentary-mcinally-why-do-united-methodists-ordain-women.

[13] "Ordination of Women," An Episcopal Dictionary of the Church, The Episcopal Church, https://www.episcopalchurch.org/glossary/ordination-of-women/.

[14] "A History of Women in the RCA," Reformed Church in America, https://www.rca.org/equipping-congregations/womens-transformation-leadership/history/#:~:text=Triennial%20gathered%20women%20for%20meaningful,Van%20Es%2C%20and%20Judy%20Nelson.

[15] Eleanor Steber, "One Little Leap At A Time," *Western Canadian Moravian Historical Magazine* 18 (April 2013), https://www.moravian.org/wp-content/uploads/sites/7/2018/10/Moravian_Historical_Magazine-No_18.pdf.

Third Wave

The third wave of feminism shifted the ideal of womanhood from the home to the workplace. No longer was the woman who stayed home to meticulously run her household, raise her children, and care for her husband considered the epitome of success. The end of the twentieth century and the start of the twenty-first century was a time that redefined a woman's place from the dining room to the board room, a trend that is perhaps most notably embodied by women such as Sheryl Sandberg and her bestseller *Lean In: Women, Work, and the Will to Lead.*

Instead of confining expectations of women's achievements to the household sphere, now women were expected to excel in all facets of life. The notion of "having it all" dominated the ways in which women—again, almost exclusively white, educated, economically stable women—were expected to approach life. These women were now expected to have an enviable life—job, family, friends, hobbies—and do it all exceptionally. This held true even if it was to the detriment of a woman's health, happiness, or wholeness.

This wave furthered a feminism that was about individual accomplishment over corporate liberation. Women with privilege had access to these accomplishments in their personal lives and public careers. But the siloing of women during this time in pursuit of their own achievements meant that progress was limited, and often the opportunities afforded to women were limited. Many women were forced to choose between personal and professional parts of their life, sacrificing significantly for elusive gain.

This wave of feminism played out in the church. Women did not have the same concrete goals to pursue as previous generations. Bylaws or regulations that kept women from pursuing ordination had been overturned. Women were granted equal access to seminary admission and ordination candidacy. Those measurable successes seemed to be in the past, and the belief that sexism was behind us persisted. But patriarchy is malleable. It worked its way through unofficial avenues.

Women who were ordained would wait longer than their male counterparts for calls and leave official leadership at rates faster than their colleagues. Those who did stay earned a portion of the salary of men, often in calls that were not full time or were relegated to staff positions formatted for ministry that would be "acceptable" for women, such as children's ministry. On average, non-white women would wait the longest for calls and earn the least.[16] All of these issues still persist.

Fourth Wave

Recent presidential election cycles have shown that white, suburban women remain a demographic with a strong pull on the culture of the country. Holding to the successes gained for them during the second and third waves of feminism—education, family, careers—they often represent the fulfillment of that specific definition of feminism. At the same time, their lives do not represent the realities of non-white people, nonbinary and transgender people, or urban and rural women. As such, these individuals with further marginalizing identities found themselves further left behind by the work of feminists in all previous eras.

As we are now in the part of history when the fourth wave of feminism is still being shaped, we have an opportunity to make something different than what has been: a version of feminism that is built on the collective liberation, the recognition of intersecting identities, and, in all things, a claiming of the truth.

Many mark the start of this wave with the #MeToo movement. In 2017, Alyssa Milano urged victims of sexual harassment to share their stories on social media with the hashtag #MeToo. (Milano was using a term originally coined in 2006 by activist Tarana Burke, who started a program called Me Too for junior high and high school students who were survivors of sexual abuse, especially non-white women.) In the first twenty-four hours, there were more than twelve million posts and comments across social media platforms.[17] Survivors of sexual assault, violence, and harassment took to these public spaces to speak the truth of what happened to them. These

[16] "45th Anniversary of the Ordination of Women—Executive Summary Clergy Questionnaire Report 2015," Evangelical Lutheran Church in America, https://download.elca.org/ELCA%20Resource%20Repository/45th_Anniversary_of_the_Ordination_Women_Lay_Full_Report.pdf.

[17] "More Than 12M 'Me Too' Facebook Posts, Comments, Reactions in 24 Hours," *CBS News*, October 17, 2017, https://www.cbsnews.com/news/metoo-more-than-12-million-facebook-posts-comments-reactions-24-hours/.

stories, mostly told by women with male perpetrators, uncovered years of unacceptable behavior from men, many in prestigious positions.

This movement spilled over into the church. Emily Joy Allison first used the hashtag #ChurchToo on social media, starting a parallel campaign to highlight the abuse found in the church. (She would go on to author a book by the same name.) In doing so, Allison broke down the wall that the church often tries to hide behind—an illusion of immunity from the ills of this world.

There are those who, instead of seeing the start of a fourth wave of feminism, believe we have entered a post-feminist time in our world. Due to the successes of previous waves, some believe that this work of liberating ourselves from patriarchy is no longer needed. After all, if there is no official barrier keeping women out of places that had been held exclusively for men, what is left to be done? The reality is that there is still so much that keeps women from being fully who they have been made and called to be in this world. And that is all the more reason this work is needed now more than ever. Fourth-wave feminism must first deal with the reality established through the successes and failures of previous waves.

A fourth wave is both underway and necessary. Considering contemporary experiences of women in our world holds the key to what it might look like to engage in a feminism that is honest, antiracist, and intersectional and advocates for the lives of all women—and by extension all people.

The first step in this work is to be honest about where we have been and what that means for our current world. We can too easily cover up these sins of the past. When we do that, we remain unable to speak truthfully about the present. There is no hope of moving forward if we refuse to be honest about the condition of our own humanity.

Next, we must recognize the impacts of intersecting identities. We must lift up and enable the accomplishments of non-white women, queer, transgender, and nonbinary leaders. Their leadership is central to defining what feminism looks like when it is embodied and creating a world where feminism is transformative in the lives of all people. We must listen to the stories of these persons, fully and completely.

When Kamala Harris spoke at the victory rally the night the 2020 presidential election was determined for Joe Biden, she said, "While I may be the first woman in this office, I will not be the last."[18] She gave this speech dressed in suffragette white at a celebration for the election of yet another white man as president. Yet her presence and election meant something was noticeably and radically different than ever before. It was most definitely a sign that patriarchy had stumbled, even if it had not fallen. For many it was also a hopeful sign of a crack in of white feminism, toward a time when we look to our sisters of all races and let them lead and guide the work of feminism that liberates all people from the patriarchal powers of this world.

But, just four years later, we saw again how well oppressive forces work together as she ran for the top seat in the country. In many ways her experience echoed that of Hillary Clinton eight years earlier. Yet Harris also had to contend with the original sin of the United States: racism. Opponents both questioned her racial identity and claimed that she was chosen only because of that identity. While her ascension to the vice presidency might have shown us what is possible, her experiences in the presidential race show us how far we still have to go.

The church is one place where this work is especially needed. In many expressions of the church, the historical truths of patriarchy, racism, homophobia, and other oppressions can loom large in comparison to other spheres of the world. It is a place where theology has created an additional barrier to breaking out of the power that patriarchy and racism have put in place. Recognizing those realities is a first step in living into a hoped-for future.

Yet the hope of fourth-wave feminism is the recognition that our liberation is bound up in the liberation of everyone else. To be free from the powers of patriarchy and all of its oppressive co-conspirators means that everyone must be free from them. The collective nature of this work is the only way forward.

Only once we are able to do these things fully and completely will we be able to build a future centered on the justice that God desires

[18] Eric Bradner and Gregory Krieg, "Kamala Harris, as First Woman Elected VP, Says She 'Won't Be the Last,'" *CNN,* November 7, 2020, https://www.cnn.com/2020/11/07/politics/kamala-harris-speech/index.html.

for all of God's people. This is the work that feminism calls us to. The purpose of this book is first and foremost to do this truth-telling work. Let us begin by being honest about what patriarchy has done and continues to do to the church today.

Chapter 2

Sanctified Silence

Silence is one of the greatest tools of the patriarchy. When sexism can go unnoticed, or at least unnamed, it holds greater power in keeping women in their societally defined places and makes surviving the limitations harder for women to navigate. To this day, the everyday-ness of sexism makes it so ubiquitous that it might seem to be the default, expected experience.

Instead of "the problem that has no name," we have created the church as yet another place in society where the problem will not be named. Lack of honesty about the presence and prevalence of sexism within the church, and within all of society, continues to be a stumbling block. While there is ample evidence and good practice of naming the effects of sexism—wage gaps, lack of female representation, and more—there is an equally strong avoidance of naming the root of the problem.

The church, like most organizations, has been constructed on the patriarchal structures that benefit most from silence around these issues. The church adds additional complications, seated deeply in theological claims and biblical understandings, and discourages questioning of such divinely inspired "truths." After all, challenging a lack of equality in the corporate world is one thing, but challenging it in a place structured in ways that claim to be ordained by God is a different problem.

While it is true that women in all spheres of life continue to experience these oppressions, there is a significant way in which theology has enabled a particular type of patriarchy to control women in the church. And one that is still permissible to share publicly, without much fear of admonition.

Around the time of my ordination, my aunt was sharing about this upcoming milestone with an acquaintance at her local gym. My aunt commented how excited she was to attend this service, as she had not previously attended an ordination, and how special it was that it would be the ordination of her niece. This fellow gym-goer was unimpressed, to say the least. She told my aunt that she did not believe women should be pastors. She went on to say that if any of her four daughters wanted to pursue a vocation in the church, she would actively discourage them from doing so. My aunt, a pediatrician, was taken aback and quickly replied that the same used to be said about women being doctors, but fortunately we have come to realize that was a ridiculous, sexist assumption.

The same is not as true beyond the church. For instance, if someone told my best friend that they did not believe she should be an attorney because she is a woman, they would be deemed as ignorant and arrogant. Moreover, if someone told her such a thing at her place of employment and acted out of that belief to limit her ability to function in her position, she would have avenues for recourse against them.

However, if the same belief is thrust on me as a clergywoman, it is deemed to be a matter of theological conviction that, even if you do not agree with it, must at least be allowed to exist. Right before Christmas a few years ago, someone visited the congregation where my husband was serving as a pastor. (This congregation is on the main line of the Philadelphia suburbs—the place where many believe the term "mainline Protestant" came to be. As you might imagine, the local towns are filled with the vast variety of the mainline Protestant denominations.) This visitor shared with him that she was looking for a new church home but that it was so hard to find something local as she did not believe women should be clergy. The news that his wife was also clergy did not sit well with her, and she did not return.

Even in denominations where the ordination of women is allowed, the ways sexism has continued to exist and impact the lives of women is profound. And that has brought us to this moment, to this work. We need to live boldly into the holy truth that there is no greater nor lesser gender identity or expression, that the lives of women are good and worthy of the same respect as men, and that we need to end the oppressive hold of sexism on the church.

When we are honest about the presence and prevalence of sexism, we can start to recognize the ways women are burdened with having to navigate around these truths.

But that is a large hurdle to clear. When sexism is named and patriarchal structures begin to crumble, it can be cause for alarm. Unsettling these systems of oppression that are meant to keep rolling can be troublesome and can remove the comfort of expectations—even when those expectations are harmful to women.

Shouldering the Blame

In addition to burdening women to navigate around the patriarchal structures of the church, women often find themselves blamed when things change. This is because the systems that operate on patriarchy can appear to fail when they are challenged for their oppressive actions. If something fails, it is in our human nature to seek out the cause and find someone or something to be at fault. When patriarchal structures are weakened, women who have called for their removal are the most vulnerable in the blame game.

Church history itself provides a strong illustration. The rise of second-wave feminism aligns, historically, with the start of the decline of Christian church attendance and engagement in local congregations throughout the United States. It is then unsurprising that some have equated the decline in participation of members to the advent of women in leadership. But the blame of women does not end there. Some have even gone as far as to equate the decline in church attendance and engagement to women collectively.

We find an example in the prominent religious historian Phyllis Tickle, who died in 2015. In early 2013, more than four hundred people gathered in Memphis, Tennessee, to honor her at a conference following the release of her book *Emergence Christianity: What It Is, Where It Is Going, and Why It Matters.* In her presentation, Tickle gave one of her fast-paced deep dives into the history of Christianity. Speaking from her perspective about the most recent change in the history of the church—the Great Emergence—Tickle discussed the historical shifts that occur every five hundred years and what is setting this current time apart from past changes.

Her presentation then took an unexpected turn. Tickle named some of the realities of the twentieth century that had impacted and shaped the lives of people in churches—particularly women—with an exploration of the medical advances that created the pill and fortified the place of birth control within society. The compounding effect, Tickle argued, was the conception of the decline of modern-day Christianity.[1]

A first-person account of Tickle's speech came from Julie Clawson, who wrote about the gathering on her blog. Clawson's summary and reflection seem to best capture the message that Tickle shared at the conference. In her review of the event, she writes:

> [Tickle] described the freedoms working outside the home in WW2 and the ability to control our cycles the Pill brought women and argued that such things led to the destruction of the nuclear family and therefore the foundation of the civil religion of Christendom. ... As she described it, when mom is not at home weaving the stories of scripture and the church calendar into her day to day activities in front of her children, they do not receive the basics of the faith. Phyllis ended the session by encouraging us to discover ways to be back in the kitchen with our children and finding crafty ways to import the rhythms of the church year to them.[2]

Tickle's claims are shocking and difficult to encounter. In essence, she states that the ability for women to control their reproductive destiny is directly related to the decline of Christianity within the

---

[1] In addition to other cited sources, description of this event based on several firsthand reports recorded in: Deborah Arca, "Emergence Christianity: A Whole Lotta Shakin' Goin' On," *Patheos*, January 8, 2013, https://www.patheos.com/blogs/faithforward/2013/01/emergence-christianity-a-whole-lotta-shakin-goin-on/; Bo Sanders, "Preferring the Past: Phyllis Tickle, Radical Orthodoxy and the Tea Party," *Tripp Fuller*, January 18, 2013, https://trippfuller.com/2013/01/18/preferring-the-past-phyllis-tickle-radical-orthodoxy-and-the-tea-party/.

[2] Julie Clawson, "Emergence Christianity, Women, and the Fall of Christendom," *onehandclapping: incantations at the edge of uncertainty*, January 14, 2013, http://julieclawson.com/2013/01/14/emergence-christianity-women-and-the-fall-of-christendom/.

United States throughout the latter part of the twentieth century. It is a bold claim. But it is also, unfortunately, unsurprising when you consider it in the context of the way patriarchy continues to seek control over all aspects of the lives of women.

Women are often the greatest perpetrators of blaming other women for seeking equity through the goals of feminism. This is, in part, because no one is exempt from the allure of oppressive structures. Women, especially those in places of societal privilege, can be beneficiaries of patriarchal structures as they support and enable other oppressions such as racism and homophobia. The patriarchy also benefits greatly from dismantling any potential shared camaraderie among women. If women are able to share experiences and realize that they are all oppressed by the same system, the system could be in jeopardy.

There is also significant anecdotal evidence that some of the harshest resistance women clergy face in the church comes from women. For example, during the 2021 Association of Teaching Theologians' Annual Convocation, three female ELCA bishops were invited to participate in a panel discussion, moderated by Karoline Lewis, a Lutheran seminary professor. This panel was part of marking the fiftieth anniversary of the ordination of women and the fortieth anniversary of the ordination of women of color in the Lutheran Church in the United States. During the panel discussion, Bishops Patricia Davenport, Patricia Lull, and Susan Candea shared their observations, challenges, and hopes for the church. When asked about how synods and seminaries might help candidates prepare to face prejudice as women, Bishop Candea shared a story of a recent experience she had while visiting a congregation in her synod. She said:

> Recently [I] had a conversation with somebody in one of our congregations—she told me she was very faithful, been to church all of her life, and she was very serious. [She] sat across from me and said, "You know what the problem with the church is, Bishop?" I said, "Share with me." [She replied,] "Women do not know their place." I said, "You do realize you

are speaking to a woman who has been a pastor for almost 38 years and is now the bishop?"[3]

This stranger thought she had diagnosed the issue threatening the success of the church in this world. Instead, she embodies the actual problem plaguing the church as well as society. At that moment she blamed women. In particular, she blamed the woman before her who serves in one of the highest places of leadership in the church and who is, in part, responsible for allowing other women to become clergy. She placed the burden of the patriarchy on a woman—a woman who has served the church in a professional leadership role for almost four decades, including as a synod bishop. While Bishop Candea countered the woman's statement, it was still her burden as a woman to do so and, in this case, her position made no difference.

Division of Labor

Simply naming the existence of the bias against women is not enough to fully understand the problems women encounter. In addition to structures that have been established and maintained for the benefit of men, other obstacles placed before women impede their ability to even make it into these structures.

In the mid-twentieth century, when women were the primary caretakers of the private realm—that is, child care and housework—it was unsurprising that the hours spent on these tasks by women far outnumbered those done by men. However, once women started entering the workplace, the statistical division of labor did not change.[4] For decades women have had to balance care for home and performance at work in ways that men have never had to fully embody. Worse still, society has attempted to convince women that they must master all aspects of life simultaneously in order to be truly successful.

For me, an experience in college taught me this unfortunate lesson. The Women's Studies Department held an annual panel

[3] "Bishops' Panel," 2021 Association of Teaching Theologians Convocation, July 26, 2021. Bishop Candea delivered these remarks during the conference. The quotation was verified by a recording of that presentation that is no longer available online.

[4] Megan Brenan, "Women Still Handle Main Household Tasks in the U.S." *Gallup*, January 29, 2020, https://news.gallup.com/poll/283979/women-handle-main-household-tasks.aspx.

discussion. Each year the question posed to the women staff and faculty panelists was the same: "Can you have it all?" As a freshman I walked away from this event frustrated. These strong, accomplished women all, in their own ways, answered this question saying, more or less, no. I was a high-achieving, motivated, young woman—furthering my mastery of balancing academics, extracurriculars, and a social life into my undergraduate career. It was upsetting to be told that there were things I would have to give up in order to fully achieve anything in life.

But as I went back each year to this panel discussion, I began to realize that these were choices only women would be forced to make. Of course, the choice disguises itself. The choice is never either/or. Instead, it is a choice for the level of engagement and commitment that one can have for all of the things that could make life fulfilling. You can have a career, a marriage, children, friendships, hobbies, and more, but you cannot expect to do them all fully or exceptionally. The panelists were right, but women continue to convince themselves of a truth that patriarchy retold and repackaged, seeking out the elusive life where they would "have it all." This only causes women to become burned out and overburdened even more.

This recognition expanded to a societal phenomenon in 2020. The COVID-19 pandemic helped to pull back the veil on many societal shortcomings; the overburdened experiences of women was one such issue. In the first six months of the pandemic, over one-third of women in heterosexual relationships in two-parent households reported doing most or all of the child care.[5] And of course, this child care looked different than ever before. In addition to the normal tasks associated with child-rearing, parent— and in this case, mothers—were forced to become teachers, librarians, cafeteria workers, study hall monitors, and recess referees. This was on top of managing their careers and all the other obligations of their livelihoods.

This reality highlighted how conditional success for women can be. In many instances it appears as though women have been given access to the same accomplishments as men. Yet these points of achievement are held away and only truly able to be obtained if a

[5] theSkimm Staff, "The State of Women."

woman can still perform or complete all of her other responsibilities as she has always done. And this is a message that women have been given throughout their whole lives.

The church, again, is no different. For millennia the church has thrived due to the labor of women—labor that has been done in unofficial and uncompensated ways. In every generation, the women have been the primary ones to provide the "homemaking" in the church. That is, they have been the ones to teach children, cook meals, clean, and prepare spaces for use.

When I was growing up my church would host an annual Mother's Day tea. For this event the men would take to the kitchen and provide the wait service. It was a striking reversal, put on display for everyone and limited to this one day a year. The novelty of this experience was celebrated rather than being held up as unveiling the patriarchy that made this event an exception when it came to how men should serve in the church.

Conditional Success

When I was young, I often reached for the movie *Cinderella*, marveling at the animal-befriending lead character who ends up with all of her dreams coming true thanks to her fairy godmother. In the movie an important scene serves as part of the rising action. When Cinderella's stepsisters, Anastasia and Drizella, are getting ready for the ball, she receives the surprising word from her stepmother that she too can attend the ball. Their conversation is as follows:

> Stepmother: Well, Cinderella, I see no reason why you can't go to the ball, if you get all your work done.
>
> Cinderella: Oh, I will.
>
> Stepmother: And if you can find something suitable to wear.
>
> Cinderella: I'm sure I can. Oh, thank you, Stepmother.
>
> Drizella: Mother, do you realize what you've just said?
>
> Stepmother: Of course. I said, "If."[6]

[6] Walt Disney, prod., *Cinderella* (Walt Disney Productions, 1950).

If. The burden on women to be forced to achieve in every sphere of life at the same time is summed up in this short, two-letter word. If women can do all of the things the world expects of them, then they can try to balance achievement outside of the domestic realm too. Cinderella would only be able to enjoy the celebrations at the ball if she could finish all of her obligations at home first. Her experience is shared throughout the lives of women. And it is a message they started hearing as little girls watching a plain yellow pumpkin turn into a golden carriage.[7]

In church leadership, this can be even more challenging for women. If women can manage the expectations of home and church, then they might be able to have space within the formal leadership of the church. In addition to the domestic obligations that women can face, women in the church are additionally burdened with making sure that all the nurturing ministries are fulfilled before they can take on administrative tasks.

A friend was in the call process with a congregation. As they approached the end of the process, she was presented with a compensation package. The male chair of the committee handed it to her with the accompanying question: "Do you want to see if your husband would like to make a counter-offer?" Every step of the process seemed as though it had been about whether she and her gifts were the right fit for this congregation. But in the end it proved to be conditional to the expectations and actions of her husband's financial decisions—even if that is not how their family unit operates. She declined the offer and did not proceed with the call process.

This story and so many others like it show that the support women receive is always within certain limits. If women are not valued highly enough for the system to make the necessary changes, then the support of women is ingenuine. And that might be the most terrible truth of all.

Lack of Genuine Support

One of the most painful facts about the impacts of sexism in the church is that support for women leadership is greatly lacking. This

[7] Richard Rogers and Oscar Hammerstein II, "Impossible," *Cinderella,* 1957, Williamson Music Company (ASCAP), Concord Music Publishing.

ranges from a lack of knowledge that women can even be clergy (I have been asked more than once if I can "even do that") to people who still do not believe that women should have authority in the church. Or, if women do have authority, they can experience people ignoring them or undermining them. Researchers Benjamin Knoll and Cammie Bolin sought to determine if the professed support of women clergy matched the reality and if that support was genuine. They published their findings in the book *She Preached the Word: Women's Ordination in Modern America.* Sadly, their work showed what many women in the church have already experienced as truth: they are not supported. More distressing is the evidence that support for women clergy is likely overreported.[8]

Sometimes this is evident in small ways. After a local Pride event, my husband and I stopped by a fast-food restaurant for a quick dinner. I was wearing a shirt that said "This Pastor Loves You" in rainbow print. My husband was in a plain T-shirt. As we stepped up to the register to place our order, the employee behind the counter looked up and said, "Nice shirt." Then, pointing to my husband he said, "Is he the pastor?"

On another occasion, my college roommate, who works as a hospital chaplain, was doing rounds and a woman stepped into the elevator she was on. The woman looked at her, noticed her clerical shirt, and said, "Well, you look like a pastor, but I know you're not." Before my roommate could respond, the doors opened and the woman stepped off.

While these are brief, fleeting moments of ignorance and arrogance, there are other times that show a deeper embeddedness of the belief that women do not deserve the authority they have rightfully earned.

When my older male colleague retired and the congregation I serve was in conversation with me about serving as the lead pastor, this issue became personal for me. One older woman in the congregation approached our council president—who was also a woman, but twenty years her junior. She told the president that she would be uncomfortable coming to me for marriage counseling because I

---

[8] Knoll and Bolin, 112.

was a woman and therefore did not feel that I should have the lead pastor position. The council president approached me, confused about the comment and slightly distressed at this lack of support for me. I assured her this type of response was sadly unsurprising—and, more so, that I hope no one expects me to offer professional marriage counseling, as that is not something I am trained to do.

I was fortunate in that this clear lack of support due to my gender was limited and resolved when this woman left the congregation. However, there are other clergy, and women in all professions, for whom the challenges to their being persist and their ability to remain in those spaces comes to an end. This is what the burden of the patriarchy on women clergy is costing the church. We are approaching a time when it will be essential to decide if that cost is worth continuing to prop up these structures that have long benefited only one portion of God's people.

Chapter 3

Her Body, Their Theology

Women constantly find themselves on the receiving end of messages about how to navigate the patriarchal structures of our society in order to survive them. This starts in messages we give young girls and intensifies as women move into more public spheres throughout their lifetime. These messages are rooted deeply in rape culture, placing the burden of protecting oneself on the potential victim. This culture sets the expectation throughout all of society for women to navigate the patriarchal structures of this world in order to avoid victimization. The same is true for women clergy in the church. The burden falls to them as the potential victims of these oppressive systems.

The reverse has not been true. Men have not been encouraged to adjust for the way that women exist. In a social media post made viral through *Feminist News*, someone wrote, "Something I heard a lot growing up: Girls, boys mature more slowly than you. Make allowances for them. Something I never heard: Boys, girls mature more rapidly than you. Look to them as examples of intelligence and leadership."[1] This illustrates a lifelong problem for women. We tell little girls that boys in class pick on them because they like them and they should therefore not only accept it but view it as a compliment. We tell teenage girls that their provocative dress will distract their classmates. We tell young women in college not to walk alone at night. We tell middle-aged women that they are past their prime. We tell elderly women that they are weak and frail. At all turns, we burden women with the expectations of others and make them adapt to those expectations.

[1] Lil Shayno from 97th, "Something I heard a lot growing up: Girls, boys mature more slowly than you. Make allowances for them. Something I never heard: Boys, girls mature more rapidly" X, September 20, 2018.

Women are well aware of the disproportionate burden they bear in order to navigate their world. We should release women from the hold of the patriarchal oppressions. But this hope seems shallow and the work too daunting. The result? Advice to women to seek a work-around, navigating for their own survival and occasional success in ways that are systematized and formalized.

Women carry these burdens, using extra effort and energy to appease the patriarchy. It reminds me of an opportunity I had in high school to go on a white water rafting trip on the Youghiogheny River in Ohiopyle, Pennsylvania. During that trip, as we approached the most dangerous rapids, there were signs along the river encouraging rafters to begin "portage." This word simply means to carry a watercraft around an obstacle—in this case, to carry our large raft along the banks of the river until we would be past the worst rapids. That is not an easy task. While the rapids might be dangerous, the path along the river is uneven and rough. And rafters must work together to carry their heavy raft, paddles, and other gear down the trail. The choice is not as simple as it seems.

These survival techniques given to women often feel like portage. The sexism that exists downriver will rock and turn your boat, attempting to toss you from your safe passage. But the work-around, portaging your raft, is hard work. There is heavy equipment to carry, and you are responsible for managing it. These paths around do not make women's lives easier. They do not help them to avoid the dangers of sexism and come out, downstream, unscathed. Instead, they require heavy lifting, hard detours, and exhausting effort. If they cannot succeed, they are seen to have failed on their journey and are criticized for their ineptitude. The burden is not on the river to change, but rather for the boaters to carry their raft until it might be safe to push off from shore again. But it never truly is.

Women clergy have been advised to find portage around the sexism that stood in their way of a safe journey. As the stories of women who live this reality are shared in the following pages, the reality of the survival techniques we have been told will emerge. For many women clergy this looks like being told to either downplay their femininity or play into feminine tropes. For others this means monitoring the way their bodies exist in public spaces, trying to change how they look to fit the expectations of others. In far too many instances, many women clergy will be victims of unwanted advances and assault. Others will have to deal intentionally with the deference to or primacy of the male experience, while still others will face the bias and accompanying comments of being or not being a mother while pastoring.

The impact of all of this is that women have altered themselves just to survive. They have left positions, sacrificed goals and compensation, worked to signal to other women what spaces are or are not safe, and live in a state of hypervigilance, constantly anticipating sexism. Regardless of the specifics of the story, the message continues to repeat and reinforce this practice of telling women how to be in a world that is not made for them to be there.

But first, we need to look at the way rape culture has shaped this part of sexist behavior toward women, including in the church.

Rape Culture

Messages given to women for how to survive patriarchy are rooted in rape culture, which is the belief that sexual violence and objectification, especially of women, is the default mode of behavior in society. Worse yet, rape culture burdens potential victims with their own survival in a world where rape is an expected experience. This is how women are instructed to live instead of working to change the culture and focusing on stopping perpetrators. If women are unsuccessful, they are often blamed.

The message is that women always need to sacrifice, to change, to remain vigilant in order to avoid being victimized. Women are told how to dress, look, and act as well as when, where, and with whom they can go in order to protect themselves. They must invest in this survival technique and live this way without the guaranteed return of safety. There is no way to escape this message and the significant implications it has for women.

This message is shared everywhere. Rape culture has seeped into all aspects of our shared life. It is present in all types of media. We see it daily on billboards, magazine advertisements, and television shows—all places where women's bodies are shown as objects used to sell things. Infamous criminal cases highlight this truth when judges are lenient on rapists so that prison sentences do not negatively impact their futures. Politicians campaign on misinformation of how women's bodies do and do not respond to the trauma of rape. And we even formalize it within our educational system—making sure that girls understand, from an early age, that this is and will be a part of their lives.

I know this was part of my own experience and that I am not unique because I went through the public school system in the United States. I remember how, one day early in the fall of my freshman year of high school, the girls from my gym class were directed to the small theater on the first floor. The boys stayed in the gymnasium. Sitting along the front of the stage was our female gym teacher and two middle-aged men who identified themselves as police detectives—something also evident by the embroidered black polo shirts they wore.

What followed was a rape and sexual assault education session—everything from naming that "boys snapping bra straps" is harassment to what to do if you are raped. The police detectives presented the circumstances that might exacerbate the likelihood of assault—such as date rape drugs in unattended drinks. The message was clear: it was our responsibility to make sure that these horrific things did not happen to us. Pay attention. Watch your drink. Do not go anywhere alone. Even if it is not the victim's fault, it is still the responsibility of the potential victim to make sure they do not have the opportunity to happen. The class period ended, and we were all sent to our third-period math class with our male counterparts. What they had been told or by whom was never discussed or known to us. As far as we knew, it was just as likely they had spent the class period playing dodgeball.

This same message to protect yourself from potential victimization is repackaged and presented to women at every turn in society. Women are advised of ways to make sure they "do not get raped" every day. Of course, this is frequently meant to be metaphorical. In the business world women are coached to control their emotions so they can get the promotion. In politics women are told to downplay their femininity so they are not seen as a bitch. The list goes on. The prevalence of these messages makes them hard to hide or ignore.

In 2018 comedian Sarah Cooper released a book titled *How to Be Successful without Hurting Men's Feelings: Non-Threatening Leadership Strategies for Women.* While this book is meant to be satirical, it is also one of those cases where something is funny because it is true. Her book includes sections such as "How to Talk Like a Man but Still Be Seen as a Woman," "How to Be Harassed Without Hurting His Career," and "Choose Your Own Adventure: Do You Want to Be Likeable or Successful?"

Cooper's message is most clearly articulated in the book's introduction:

> So arm yourself with the knowledge of these pages, ladies. Be vigilant about hiding yourself. (Not your entire self, just the woman and/or minority part of yourself.) Scale the heights of your career and break the glass ceiling, but do it very quietly and gingerly, and be sure to make a man think he did it for you. By standing as still as possible, you will go farther than you ever imagined, as long as you didn't imagine going too far.[2]

Cooper's book goes to the extent of codifying what has been known and experienced by women for generations. Someone somewhere will show up to tell you how to live in order to help maintain the patriarchy. Cooper's book pulls back the veil on that process and puts it out in front of everyone to examine. If, as she states, it is a woman's responsibility to navigate the world so as to maintain the well-being of men, then why not create a manual so the process can be clear and concise and, perhaps, even more effective? If that seems absurd, then maybe that is an invitation to consider how we have arrived at this place within our shared life, at least, that is Cooper's hope.

---

[2] Sarah Cooper, *How to Be Successful Without Hurting Men's Feelings: Non-Threatening Leadership Strategies for Women* (Kansas City, MO: Andrew McMeel Publishing, 2018), 5.

Another example comes from the viral social media question posed to women in the spring of 2024, asking: Would you rather be stuck in the woods with a man or a bear? Almost without exception, women who responded chose the bear. The reasons? "The bear won't tell you to act like you like it." "The bear's friends won't lie to vouch for him if you survive and tell somebody what he did to you." "As so many of us women were raised to believe, there are some fates worse than death. The bear will deliver death. A man can deliver so much worse."[3]

Kate Lister, a feminist historian, wrote an article responding to this question. In her piece she wrote, "I want to say 'the man,' I really do, but I can't shake the idea that I would be safer with the bear. … The beauty of the question lies in its vagueness because it forces you to work with averages. On average, is a woman safer in the woods with a man or a bear?"[4] After the publication of her piece, Lister received a barrage of vitriolic messages from men telling her that she had made the wrong choice. She then shared this message on social media: "Since writing this article, I have received messages from angry men, calling me names, telling [me] I'm wrong, [and] that I'd be begging a man to save me if I was lost in the woods. To recap, there are men sending me abusive emails to prove they are the safe choice. So far, no bears have written in."[5]

Those who benefit from the power of this culture become angry when something attempts to disrupt the hold they have over others.

---

[3] Amber Wardell, "Why Women Say They'd Choose the Bear: A Non-Comprehensive List," *Medium*, May 2, 2024, https://medium.com/@amber_wardell/why-women-say-theyd-choose-the-bear-a-non-comprehensive-list-b35b2e0d60bb.

[4] Kate Lister, "Women, Would You Rather Be Stuck in a Forest with a Man or a Bear?" *The i Paper*, April 23, 2024, https://inews.co.uk/opinion/women-rather-stuck-forest-with-man-bear-3019615?fbclid=IwY2xjawLkZ5ZleHRuA2FlbQIxMQBicmlkETFOOG4wcGFlTncyOFkwNXJhAR5xEJvNM_aqB40IaqXOzCax-zvaDPm7kIbHVXD4-XlGiGP9-5g2gh0-TLNe8g_aem_85pqie5p4cyUJhGbalfcDg.

[5] Kate Lister (@k8lister.bksy.social), "Since writing this article, I have received messages from angry men, calling me names, telling I'm wrong, & that I'd be begging a man to save me if I was lost in the woods. To recap, there are men are sending me abusive emails to prove they are the safe choice. So far, no bears have written in," Bluesky, April 29, 2024, https://bsky.app/profile/k8lister.bsky.social/post/3krcbkos4mk2j.

Rather than using the fact that women are choosing the bear—an animal known for its predatory ways—as an opportunity to consider why that might be, the patriarchal systems respond in a way to protect themselves—even if that means further perpetuating the attacks on women to maintain their power.

Purity Culture

While these examples are based in the secular parts of our world, the church is also culpable in perpetuating this message to women. To know that the church plays a role in keeping this culture in place is disheartening and, in many cases, dangerous for women—dangerous because it wraps these unhealthy and violent actions toward women in scripture and theology, claiming it to be pleasing to God.

One of the most public versions of rape culture within the church is "purity culture." There is an expectation that women should remain "pure"—typically defined as remaining a virgin until marriage. This purity culture, originating primarily from the evangelical movement of the last part of the twentieth century, focuses on controlling women's bodies, specifically around issues of sexuality. Religious communities that purport this purity messaging will make young girls pledge their purity to their fathers, typically symbolized by a ring, until they are presented as virginal brides to their grooms. This is one of the most extreme examples of the burden placed on women. There is no equivalent expectation for men to remain virgins until their marriage, at least not formally constructed like it is for women. There is also the expectation that the groom will be able to have sex with a virgin on his wedding night. The same is not true for the bride.

Mainline Protestant denominations embody these expectations and a version of purity culture of their own making, upholding rape culture in their own ways. Until recently, my denomination held to a document of moral standards for clergy that included statements that unmarried clergy would remain chaste.[6] The same is true in other denominations. The belief is that uprightness of character and

[6] In March 2020, the ELCA Church Council voted to remove "Vision and Expectations" from its governing documents. "ELCA Church Council Votes to Remove 'Vision and Expectations,'" Evangelical Lutheran Church in America, March 8, 2020, https://elca.org/News-and-Events/8027.

morality is tied to the sexuality and sexual experiences of clergy—especially women, for whom there is a telling result if birth control fails.

What does this look like in the everyday lives of female pastors? Rev. Sara Miller said, "I got married a year earlier than we intended so that we did not have to sneak [my now-husband] in and out of the parsonage every time he came to visit. When I asked what exactly had prompted their change in wedding plans, she shared this story:

> I asked the personnel committee whether my fiancé could stay with me at the parsonage in one of my multiple extra bedrooms (it was just my dog and me in a giant house). He lived in a different part of the country and wanted to visit for Holy Week both because it was his academic spring break and he wanted to support me professionally. We couldn't afford to put him up in a hotel for eight days. The personnel committee said no but suggested that he spend each night with a different parishioner so they could get to know him. When I said that wouldn't work, they then hit upon the idea that one of the single church members could spend the week in the parsonage with us as our chaperone. That church member was a teacher who would also be on spring break that week. I quickly arranged for my fiancé to "stay" at a colleague's house. This other pastor was also a single woman, but since she was not dating him, the personnel committee was fine with that. Then we snuck him in and out of my house for that week.

The expectations of purity culture are on full display within this congregational system in how they sought to control their pastor and any experience that could be seen as sexually illicit. This is not a standalone experience. Other women clergy worry where a significant other parks their car while visiting and if their partner who lives out of town can attend morning worship since that could mean they spent the night. This is how the church, even in liberal denominations, seeks to control women's bodies.

Women clergy are especially among those who are taught—formally and informally—how to survive the patriarchal structures of the church that want to forcefully take dignity and autonomy away from them. In these controls of our bodies, how we present them, how we use them, how we do or do not parent, all comes together to be placed on our shoulders. Meanwhile, no suggestion is made that the church should change its expectations. The fear of losing power tightens the grip around patriarchy. The easier alternative is to sacrifice the lives of women for the stability of the institution.

The next chapter will be filled with the messages women clergy have been given. The everyday realities of women clergy will be shared by weaving in the stories of my colleagues who graciously shared these vulnerable experiences with me. While it is difficult to wade through the weight of these stories, it is important to know the ubiquity of them. These messages will highlight the constant burden placed on women and will also uncover the ways the church offers up the lives of women to maintain the patriarchy.

Chapter 4

Echoes in the Sanctuary

This chapter is the heart of the matter. The pages ahead include stories from women clergy who have entrusted me with their experiences for the purpose of sharing them in this space. These stories also represent many other women and echo the lives of so many in the church. I am grateful for the vulnerability and bravery of those who have stepped forward to share their experiences.

To collect these stories I first posted in the private Facebook group of Young Clergy Women International to invite the sharing of these stories through comments or conversation. In less than twenty-four hours there were nearly one hundred comments on the thread. It became heartbreaking to read, despite affirming what I had witnessed and suspected to be true. Women do not need to think long and hard to come up with these examples. We live with these realities every day and have more than enough stories to tell. Often, the comments on the thread were accompanied with phrases like "there are so many" or "this is just a sample" or "just in this past week." Other women clergy affirmed the stories with responses like "I've experienced this as well" and "that happened to me too."

That post led to correspondence, conversations, and interviews with clergywoman after clergywoman. They all echoed the same problem: never in their ordained ministry had there been a time free from the oppressions of sexism. This issue is not an isolated phenomenon nor the experiences of a few individuals; rather, it is a still-present and active limitation of clergywomen and the work they are called to do in this world.

Navigating the Double Bind

I have heard it said that there is no "perfect" for women. They are either too young or too old, too beautiful or too unattractive, too strong or too weak. This creates the environment that generates the greatest amount of advice to women to help them adjust to meet the expectation they are missing. This is the basis for messages like "Wear a little makeup," "Try to smile more," and "Don't show so much skin." Women are always too much of something or not enough of another thing. They are constantly told how to adjust in a fruitless search for that perfect balance.

In the 2023 summer blockbuster *Barbie,* the main (human) protagonist articulates this issue as a root cause of the problems women experience in the world. Gloria, played by America Ferrera, gives a soliloquy at the climax of the film expressing her frustration with this truth. She says, in part:

> It is literally impossible to be a woman. … We have to be skinny, but not too much and you must not say you want to be skinny. … You must have money, but you can't ask for money because that would be rude. You gotta be a boss, but you can't be tough. You must lead, but you cannot crush other people's ideas. … You have to be a professional, but also always take care of everyone else. You are responsible for men's misbehavior, which is crazy, but if you notice that, you're accused of being a whine. You're expected to keep yourself pretty for men, but not so pretty you "try them too much" or threaten other women, because you're supposed to be part of the sorority. It's very hard, it's too contradictory, and nobody gives you a medal or says thank you. And it turns out, in fact, that not only are you doing everything wrong but also, everything that happens is your fault. I'm tired of seeing myself and every woman doing the impossible for others to love us.[1]

This became the most shared scene from the movie on social media. It struck a chord that women across the country understand

[1] *Barbie*, directed by Greta Gerwig, featuring Margot Robbie and Ryan Gosling (Warner Brothers, 2023).

deep in their bones.[2] They know there is a trap. They can never be too much of one thing or not enough of another and survive. Yet that is the expectation placed before them.

When it comes to leadership, the challenge is even greater to navigate. Women are easily seen as too dominant or not assertive enough.

Simply put, women are caught in a double bind between two irreconcilable options for how to act in this world.

The result is that women are given tactics to navigate around, to change how they lead, to employ tactics that highlight or downplay the expectations of whether women should or should not be in these scenarios. Clergywomen find themselves in this predicament especially when it comes to seeking out calls to serve the church. There is a belief that a female candidate will be "too much" or "not enough." The advice that is often and readily given is to play up or downplay our femininity. For example, there is a belief that nurturing ministries—things like work with children and youth or pastoral care—are better suited for women. To that end, some women are encouraged to play up that part of their identity in order to land a specified call to these types of work. Typically, these are associate positions in larger congregations.

When I was in the call process for what would eventually become my first call, an older female colleague cautioned me. The call was a staff position—an associate pastorate with an older male colleague. She told me that I would be expected to "just take care of the children and youth ministry and handle all of the pastoral care" and that I should want more than that. I did not know how to reply. After all, those things gave me joy in parish ministry, and this position held the ability for me to focus on my strengths and serve in my favorite areas of congregational life.

I have since come to understand her words of advice. In her opinion, I was being limited to the areas of ministry that would be "acceptable" for a woman to do. Her own experience and the ways

[2] Sophie Caldwell, "Read the 'Barbie' Monologue that Provoked Such an Emotional Reaction Among Viewers," *Today,* August 2, 2023, https://www.today.com/popculture/movies/america-ferrara-barbie-monologue-full-text-reaction-rcna96237.

she had been relegated to this specific type of work throughout her ministry made her wary of what would happen to clergywomen coming after her. I felt the opposite and was excited to live into this role that felt like it had been made for me. Of course, there is the possibility that I am orientated toward this type of ministry because I was socialized and conditioned as a woman to seek these nurturing types of roles. But that is a separate issue of the permeation of the patriarchy into every space it can find and well beyond what we can consider here.

This challenge was a repeated story from my colleagues about their own call processes. Over and over again women clergy were told that these were the types of positions they should expect or, in some cases, the best they could hope to get. This is tied to both the way these types of positions are considered acceptable roles for women and the way they keep women out of positions of power. My fellow clergywomen shared these reflections in response to my post:

> Rev. Sandy Harris: I was told this: "Don't aim too high, you won't get a pastorate right off," and, "Don't dream about the big steeple churches, look at the smaller churches."
>
> Rev. Mary Lewis: I was told that, because I was a woman, I would be more likely to get an associate minister position right out of seminary.
>
> Rev. Lisa Walker: At the place I did my required psych evaluation, the female psychologist told me if I wanted to get married and have a family I would only be able to serve as an associate and not to even consider solo ministry. She even wrote that in her report to my [ordination panel].
>
> Rev. Jessica Young: When in the call process for my previous call as an associate, a member said, "We only voted to call you because the call committee chair and senior pastor promised that you would never be the senior pastor."

Of course, playing up your femininity to land a position will only get you so far. It will also make you vulnerable to other comments as people try to limit the display of women in authority in the church. When women take positions to be acceptable to their gender, it becomes part of the performative nature of gender. Women continue to be objectified—especially for their bodies. The way the church's expectations of these displays of femininity and female sexuality sets up the next trap for women clergy to attempt to avoid.

Body Politics

There are times when hiding our own femaleness becomes the prescribed path forward. Rev. Abigail Jones was told that when she entered a congregation she would do so with "three strikes against her'" as she was young, single, and female. While not explicitly stated, it would be hard to do much about the first two, but downplaying femininity could help adjust the congregation's perception of their new pastor.

This is not surprising, as patriarchy always seeks to control women's bodies. When women enter public spaces, the impetus for sexism to control how women look in those spaces increases. That can be a multi-billion-dollar industry because it is never about the specifics of what women should or should not wear, but rather the behaviors that are shaped by society's messages. This is the effort of the capitalistic society, at the behest of patriarchy and other oppressions, to teach women how to behave. In other words, this is a way for society to dictate that women should adjust their appearance to make them more "acceptable." This means keeping up with the current fashions, investing in the latest beauty craze, and seeking after the unattainable.

A great historical illustration of this is the role of pockets in women's clothing and the relationship to first-wave feminism. These changes in fashion paralleled the freedoms women were seeking in other realms. At the turn of the twentieth century, suffragettes began advocating for pockets to be added on women's clothes.[3] Prior to this, pockets were reserved for men's clothing—a sign of their place in the public realm where they would need to carry something in and out of the world outside the home. So, in addition to the right to vote and other political positions, pockets became a hallmark of the women's movement in that era. This would come to be known as

[3] Chelsea G. Summers, "The Politics of Pockets," *Vox*, September 19, 2016, https://www.vox.com/2016/9/19/12865560/politics-of-pockets-suffragettes-women.

the "suffragette suit"—complete with no fewer than six pockets. In their pockets these protesting women could stash their pamphlets that spoke of subversion and how to gain the right to vote. They wore, as poet Sharon Owens says, "dangerous coats, made of pockets & sedition."[4]

While this example might seem not to connect much to the realities of life for women today, any woman who has ever shopped for clothes knows does. To this day, the inclusion of pockets in women's clothing remains novel. Sometimes faux pockets are sewn onto garments for appearances, and those that are functional are typically much smaller than the ones placed in men's clothing. Compliment a woman's outfit that has adequate pockets, and more often than not she will thank you and put her hands in her pockets to show you the truth, inviting you to marvel at the reality of this simple act of subversion. This is because of the centuries of controlling women's bodies through controlling the way fashion might complement, accentuate, or just make a garment functional.

Instead of the specific example of limiting pockets, women in churches and particularly women clergy are expected to "cover up." That is, women clergy are expected to embody a certain level of modesty lest they tempt any of their male parishioners into focusing on something other than God. As one pastor noted, this typically means wearing something "black and shapeless." Women clergy constantly receive messages that their attractiveness needs to be altered. This comes through both explicit messages ("Pushing your bangs out of your face while you were preaching distracted me from what you were saying") to unwanted attention ("I just love watching you move up there in the pulpit"). Both of these statements were shared with me in various iterations by several women clergy. As a result, alterations to their appearance become the topic of conversations after worship. Instead of "nice sermon," women are told "nice haircut."

Far more than male colleagues, women clergy are constantly aware of what they are wearing and who is watching. Rev. Ruth Miles

[4] Shannon Owens, "Dangerous Coats," X, November 26, 2020, https://twitter.com/womensart1/status/1332088490012667908?lang=en.

shared this experience of balancing the clothes she needed to wear for her position—working with youth, which required a more casual wardrobe—and what the older women of her church expected all women to wear: her Sunday best. She tells her experience and how her supervisor tried to solve this problem for her future self:

> When I was a twenty-something-year-old youth minister/pastor intern I had to carry extra clothes in my car because the older women would give me dirty looks and not speak to me—which was a nonverbal way of letting me know that I didn't dress appropriately. [My supervisor] bought me a very loose-fitting, shapeless, horrible, probably men's alb, as a parting gift. His idea was that it would be helpful for me to navigate the clothing issues as I go on in my ministry career by essentially eliminating the problem. They can't judge my clothes if they don't see them. It's hideous and absolutely useless, especially since my tradition doesn't wear albs!

Even then, efforts to maintain the expected modesty or unattractiveness are not always enough. A story that has been shared throughout multiple clergy groups is that of a woman who, on her first Sunday in her parish, was approached by a man who smirked at her and asked, "Do you wear anything under that robe?" This story is almost handed down in warning to the next generation of women clergy of the messages they might, but sadly probably will, get.

The objectification of their bodies is the source of an unending barrage of angry, incredulous, sorrowful comments from women. There is no way to fully articulate the way these comments feel violating to the women who receive them. Once, at a community event hosted by my congregation, an older man I did not know came up to me and asked if I was a pastor at the church. I said yes and braced myself for what I assumed he would say next—something about me being too young to be a pastor or wondering how women pastor. Instead, he pointed at my older male colleague and asked if he too was a pastor at the church. I said yes. He turned back to me and said, "I'd much rather watch you up there than him." While I wish I had called out this man's sexism, I am grateful that I had the strength to turn and walk away without feigning politeness. Regardless of how I responded,

I was burdened with what to do with it. He had not burdened any man with this inappropriate thought. He had not approached my male colleague to share the opposite comment. Like in all things of the patriarchy's making, the lot falls to women to endure these experiences because of the way they are constructed to be not-men.

This problem persists far beyond unwanted comments. The most significant way that rape culture has seeped into the pews of our churches is when women's bodies are violated. Not only do they endure harassment and assault, but they have not found support from their church in pursuing justice or guaranteed freedom of repeat violations. Rev. Tara Smith shared this story:

> In my exit interview from my first call, I told them that while I knew for a variety of reasons I wouldn't stay long, the thing that pushed me to leave more quickly was an experience of sexual harassment from church members (and really only one person in that church was equipped with the knowledge, understanding, and power to help me address that). The response of the (older clergywoman) committee chair? "I'm sorry that happened to you. And I'm sorry I can't promise it won't happen somewhere else." She wasn't wrong that she can't promise that I won't experience harassment elsewhere. But she did not seem to understand the important difference between a context where that kind of behavior is largely tolerated (and seen as a harmless joke) and one where the majority of the leadership would understand that the behavior was unacceptable.

Despite acknowledging the problem with the offer of sympathy, this older clergywoman simultaneously showed her own resignation to the fact that this can (and far too often will) happen again in the church.

Another pastor, Rev. Jennifer Sanders, talked about how she had been conditioned to stay quiet about such things throughout the time in her training congregations, so she did not come "out swinging" when she became a victim. On her first Sunday of her first call, she was groped during the passing of the peace by a man in the congregation. This would continue throughout her time at that congregation, being the recipient of repeated inappropriate touch by more than one male member. It became increasingly difficult, as time passed, to bring up this issue and create a path forward within the congregation. Her physical safety was compromised to keep the status quo of the congregation. But that is often the way women are taught to be and how to survive. After all, the perpetrators of this assault are men and are excused for their actions: "Boys will be boys." The "rights" of men to act this way are valued above women's rights to safety.

The Second Sex

Women come second. The needs of men are placed first, and women receive what is left available for them in the otherness of their identity. Men are viewed as the standard, the default experience of the human experience. Women are placed in relation to this assertion. The church, like all structures that benefit from the oppression of women, makes the default experience that of men. There is always the need to qualify the reality of women clergy as it is seen as "other." Women clergy live with this constantly, ranging from everyday microaggressions about their authority to systemic procedures that prioritize the leadership of their male colleagues.

Even though my former colleague and I had the same position title of "pastor," anyone who met us assumed that, because he was an older male and I a younger female, he was the "senior pastor" and I was the "associate pastor." This is the most basic way in which this issue of being second plays out. The assumption of greater authority gets allotted to men. This is the same bias that has forced or limited women to hold positions deemed less valuable or only work in ministry areas that are "appropriate" for their gender. Or it results in situations like the woman who left my congregation because she would not feel comfortable coming to me for marriage counseling because of my gender.

This is a nearly everyday occurrence for women—and clergy might have a particularly greater occurrence, as denominations that do not allow for the ordination of women hold power over the public narrative of what a pastor looks like. A few years into my first call, I was in the lobby of the church setting up some things for the coming Sunday. I was wearing a simple summer dress, as I often do during the warmer months—especially as I typically only wear clerics for Sundays and other official pastoral responsibilities. As happens each year, the Gideons came around on their annual visit. The two older men walked through the front door, looked at me, and asked, "Is the pastor here?" This was not the first nor the last time I was asked if *the* pastor was available. Sometimes it was because they did not know I was a pastor. Other times it was because my colleague was called "Pastor" and my name became a qualifier, making me "Pastor Alina." This particular situation remains in my memory because of the way I used their sexism as a way out of a conversation I did not want to have. I told them the pastor was not in and I did not know when *he* would be returning.

When the male experience is used as the norming experience, men can easily be perceived as the experts. This is especially true in fields that have historically been theirs to rule—like the church. Women are told to be more like their male colleagues. This is even if those habits are unhealthy—such as overworking, having a lack of boundaries, and compromising life outside of the church for the sake of one's career. Rev. Stephanie Quinn shared her experience in her current parish. The striking thing about her story is that the man who is seen as the expert is not present in the system currently. She shared this: "I'm a new priest (perceived to be young and naive despite being nearly forty), and I have a recent diagnosis of ADHD. I am constantly encouraged to speak to the former rector about time management and balancing workload." There is no impetus in the congregation to offer the support for this particular person with her particular needs, only a desire to point her to a man who can "help" her.

Another prevalent theme in the comments from colleagues centered around the experiences of heterosexual clergy couples and the way the male spouse was prioritized. This often means that the female spouse could be left without call prospects until her spouse has successfully secured a position—even if he wasn't looking for one. Pastor Samantha Neale shared this experience:

> Every time I'd put my paperwork in and ask for a new call they would send my husband paperwork and then tell me once they had him settled they would find something for me. He wasn't looking to take a new call. So my mobility options

> were nonexistent for years. We once were sent paperwork for two congregations working toward merging, and it was assumed he would take the larger, healthier congregation and I would take the other.

Like so many areas of life, the experiences of women are undervalued and those of men are prioritized. They are used as the norm and the norming. The structures then push out any experience that does not fit that of men. This is true even when considering something that only women can do: bear children.

The Motherload

Many of the stories told to me by my female colleagues involved their pregnancy or parenting. Despite a fairly common belief throughout congregations in a natural church growth method that involves people in the church having children to raise in the faith, this becomes increasingly complex when the pastor is the one having the children. Women are often told they need to choose between motherhood and their careers—especially careers that are considered to be a "man's job." As one of my closest colleagues, Pastor Melanie Stone, was asked, "Why do you think you can be a pastor and a mother?" Men would never be forced to think that a calling to both ministry and parenthood is beyond their capabilities. Yet women frequently receive this message and are told to adjust their expectations or the way they do one of those callings for the sake of the other.

When women step into the public realm, any part of their life that is meant for the private realm cannot exist supported in both spaces. These are the instances where women will most appear to "fail." Their inability to manage the private and the public simultaneously will be held up and used against them as a reason they should not try to do both. The patriarchy uses this way to control the lives of women and the construction of motherhood. When women try to be both pastor and mother, the lines of the public and the private become blurred. The patriarchy will always work to relegate women back to the private, the home, the childbearing roles that work to maintain the benefits of the public realm being for men.

Before I further exploration of this topic, I want to clearly name my relationship to this issue. I am intentionally a non-parenting woman. (I prefer the term "non-parenting" to "childless" or "child-free," as I do not feel called to a life that excludes children in my family, life, and work in the church.) I have never felt called to motherhood, and I made a deliberate choice not to birth or adopt children into my family unit, but I will be the first to tell you how incredible my niece and nephew are! I also make no secret of this decision. If people inquire about children in my life, I share that I do not want to be a parent.

My first call included being the primary pastor for children and youth ministry. When people in my congregation witnessed me interacting with the young members and doing it well, they naturally concluded that I would someday want children of my own. When I am told things like "you will be a great mom," I respond that I do not plan on being one. I also let them know that being good at working with children is not the same as being good at raising them. There is often a shocked reaction; and I have been told, more times than I like, that I will change my mind (and hopefully before it is too late). But when I hear from my colleagues about the challenges and blatant sexism they have received in relation to their children, it is clear that the church would never be a factor in changing my mind to have a child.

The times women clergy have shared about the way they are treated and, often by extension, the way their children are treated, are some of the most terrible examples of the rampant sexism in our world. More often than not, these stories include committees, policies, and congregation-wide expectations far above other examples explored. Rather than one person telling the pastor after church about her hair, these oppressions are systematized.

The absence or meager presence of parental leave policies is one of the greatest indicators of the congregation's values around supporting a pastor who is called to parent, especially women. Far too often, women clergy are told that the church will "figure out" a parental leave policy *if* it is needed, rather than clearly defining it at the time the pastor starts the call. This represents a hope from the congregation that such things will never be needed. After all, that means that the church will have to pay for their pastor to be at home caring for a child rather than at the office doing her job.

A few years ago, I heard of a pastor who served a church that did not have a parental leave policy in place at the time she took the call. When she shared with the congregation leadership that she was pregnant and due in December, they told her she could take two weeks of unpaid parental leave following the birth of her first child so that she would be back in time for Christmas services. (After all, what is Christmas about if not the inconveniencing of a postpartum mother and her newborn child?) She did not stay at the call long past that incident. Her story is not the anomaly we might wish it was.

Rev. Julie Maxwell shared this similar experience:

> The council refused to discuss my parental leave until I was eight months pregnant, at which point they said comments such as, "What will we do when people die?!" (insinuating that I can't actually take leave and have to come back for funerals, or that being gone made me a bad pastor) and, "We didn't have this problem when we had a male pastor." They made complaints about paying for [my leave], even though part of it was unpaid and they would literally save money. I took the leave, and when I returned two weeks before Christmas as I had agreed, they suggested (or rather "decided") I would not lead Christmas Eve worship but insisted I just come and enjoy time "with the family" because they wanted to meet the baby. When I confronted these behaviors in a council meeting, one member asked me when I was going to baptize the child, saying, "We can't wait to have a baptism here!" as if they had not called my daughter "a problem." When I resigned from that call, rumors were spread about me that I had a mental illness and it must be postpartum depression. The very same community that made baptismal promises to support and raise my first child in the faith could not seem to hold space for my second child to simply exist without being objectified. The violation of this spiritual trust by a particular community in the Body

> of Christ caused an invisible and painful spiritual trauma that I had to carry on my shoulders for years to come. Only after years of counseling and healing did I have the emotional capacity to learn to trust God's people in a pastoral relationship again.

Sadly, but unsurprisingly, these issues persist far past the initial parental leave time. Women clergy are told that their children will distract them from their job and that they are not allowed to have their children in the church office. Pastor Elizabeth Williams said, "I was told that my daughter's presence was a distraction. But only during the week. Sundays she was 'theirs.'" During the week a child in the church is a distraction to her mother, while on Sunday the child is part of the church community led by a pastor. The division of the private and the public persists and always to the detriment of women.

Two women clergy shared stories of messages about their children that turned into official messaging and policy within their churches. This formalization of sexism makes it harder to change cultures, harms the women whose lives these policies or committees are in response to, and sets an unhealthy precedent for all those who will come next. These stories highlight this:

> Rev. Victoria Wilson: While on parental leave … [a] committee chair called me at suppertime/feeding time to discuss a church business matter. My baby was screaming the whole time, as honestly it was bottle time which I was trying to do. This led to an official email from [the personnel committee] stating I was never to bring my daughter to work because it was unprofessional and distracting. It still grinds on me three years later, as she had called me when I was on leave to do work.

> Rev. Morgan Anderson: The senior pastor, who was an older, white man close to retirement, brought in [the personnel committee] to tell me how my children were distracting me from doing my job and that my children should not be allowed in my office anymore because they were keeping me from doing my work. They didn't want me to have any of my kids' toys or anything in my office. There was an expectation

to keep the professionalism of the pastorate separate from the realities of being a mom.

This bias against women in relation to choosing to be a mother happens well before they have children and well outside of whether there are policies in place to support these women. While asking about the prospect of having children in an interview is a poor decision, legally speaking, the prevalence of these questions in call interviews at churches is undeniable. But then again, churches are not beholden to the same legal boundaries around such issues. If a woman does not have children, she will be asked when she plans to have them. If she has them, she will be asked how she plans to manage them. The same is not true for men when they are interviewing for positions. I heard this story from Pastor Olivia Brown about when she and her husband were both interviewing for their first calls:

> As someone in a young clergy couple, when we were both interviewed for possible first calls, I was asked multiple times in different ways how having children will make my job as pastor more difficult and why should that not be a con of calling me versus my husband. He was never asked anything about children in interviews, of course.

While I have, thankfully, never been questioned in an interview about having children, I often wonder if because I do not want to have children my truthful response would make me a more attractive candidate. It is heartbreaking to consider that my choices would put me above other women instead of honoring all of us for the ways we have followed our individual callings to shape our lives.

When women are forced to choose between themselves and the church, both lose. When children are involved, the situation becomes far more precarious. But the patriarchy does not care which lives are sacrificed for the sake of maintaining power. Women and children will not be put on the lifeboats first; the lives of men are the ones saved when everything else is sinking.

Chapter 5

The Cost of Her Discipleship

No matter what consideration is given to the impacts of this messaging to women, there is no way to truly capture the pain, emotional distress, loss of career and financial opportunities, and trauma that are caused by these situations that have been described so far. Despite the recognition of this inability to capture fully the way this affects women, it is still necessary to name and explore them insofar as is possible. Women clergy live with the burden of having to survive these systems: being forced to choose between leaving their positions or accepting the experiences of sexism, signaling safety to others, and hypervigilance, constantly anticipating sexist behavior.

The church will far too often force women to choose. Sometimes that choice means loss of job, loss of financial stability, or loss of relationships. Women are pressed to show their allegiance to the institution, to the oppressive structures that wish to remain intact. If it is perceived that they are unable to do so and that there is another priority in their life, they will be forced to make a choice.

When these situations force a decision between the church and family, the reality of the public-versus-private strain on a woman's life becomes apparent. This is the desire of the public realm to make it look like a woman has failed and needs to return to the private realm. This strain impacts not just a woman, but also the relationships in her life outside of her work. Rev. Sophia Davis, in talking about the difficult position she was placed in balancing the expectations of her older male colleague as well as the family life she was called to share, found the very real pain of this choice. She said, "It was not only hurting my marriage but my family so much. We got to the point where if we didn't get out I would have not only left ministry, I probably would have ended up divorced because of the stress it was putting on my family." She was unwilling to choose her career over her family and left that position, and subsequently that denomination.

The consequences are significant. The cost to the pastor and the church is significant, but patriarchal structures convince the church that the cost is bearable. Pastor Emma Johnson shared this reflection: "I have recently been diagnosed with PTSD from this experience, while getting my neurodivergence diagnosed. I don't know if I will ever feel safe in the church again. Not only did this have emotional, spiritual, and physical consequences, but significant financial consequences." In this instance, like so many, the woman pastor had to sacrifice so much in order to simply survive.

The other choice is to live with the treatment, accepting sexism as an unwanted guest who refuses to leave. This option comes with compromising oneself to maintain systems. Women, especially women pastors, are expected to be "nice," and even more than that, they need to keep the men happy. In other words, they are told they just need to deal with the treatment for the sake of the church and their ability to continue in ministry. Two colleagues shared their experiences with that very situation:

> Rev. Charlotte Taylor: After months of verbal abuse and eventually shady conspiratorial firing by the new head of staff pastor, a liaison from the [denomination's judicatory] met with me alone, where she told me I would need to "bend over backwards and learn to stroke men's egos" if I wanted to stay in ministry.

> Rev. Ava Jackson: I got the message pretty strongly that sexism and misogyny was something I would just have to learn to cope with because, even if I thought they were theologically wrong, to argue directly with a parishioner about complementarianism or the role of women in the church would be disrespectful. So I just had to deal with it.

These choices are never fair and force a compromise in the lives of those who are confronted with them. It means losing your calling or losing yourself. One of the ways women have been forced to survive is to make note of the places in this world that force these decisions more than others. They know well the places that have been supportive and those that want them to push themselves aside for the sake of the church. They know these things, and they work to share that information with others.

Women often resort to signaling to others in trusted circles which spaces are or are not safe. Frequently, when I see job postings shared in groups of clergywomen, they mention whether male colleagues will treat someone in that position well. I know I have done the same. When speaking of my former older, male colleague, I often refer to him as "one of the good ones." This means that he respected me and my authority publicly and privately, assumed he and I both had gifts to share with each other, and championed and advocated for me when I was not met with the same treatment by others.

I know I am in a small and privileged minority for young women clergy who have worked with older male clergy and count it as a positive relationship. I heard the same reflected in 2018 when Pastor Andrea Roske-Metcalfe wrote "Do & Don't: An Open Letter to Older Male Senior Pastors Regarding Your Working Relationships with Younger Women/Femme/Non-Binary Associate Colleagues." This post was shared widely among women clergy. In the opening paragraphs of her letter, Roske-Metcalfe wrote this:

> Several months ago I received a phone call inviting me to speak on a panel to a cohort of women clergy who met monthly. Several of them were associate pastors, struggling mightily with how to claim any authority at all in their respective ministry settings.
>
> The facilitators were inviting me, they said, because I was an "outlier" in my own call; the relationship between my older male colleague and I was understood to be an anomaly because we functioned as partners more than anything. They knew that we shared a genuine, mutual respect and that we actually enjoyed our working relationship. They knew that I exercised considerable agency and authority in my role, and that my colleague supported me in that, rather than being threatened by it. They knew that we pushed each other to be better, more authentic, and more courageous in our pastoral

> identities, and that both our congregation and the wider community were benefiting as a result.
>
> Let that sink in for a minute—my pastoral colleague and I have a functional working relationship built on mutual respect, and we enjoy each other's company. That makes us outliers.[1]

After I read this article, I shared it with my older male colleague and thanked him for making us outliers too. But both of our hearts broke for so many for whom this is not true. At the end of her letter, Roske-Metcalfe admits that when it is time to seek a new call she will not be open to another associate position. She writes, "I am not naïve. I have been paying attention for the better part of a decade to what this particular kind of call does to so many people, and I know how rare my situation is, even if I don't think it should be. I would rather do this work on my own than be treated as anything less than I am."[2]

I heard this repeated in conversations with my colleagues. The ways they are treated by older colleagues, particularly men, are unacceptable. But they are forced to work around them, and in solidarity with other women they work to signal where women clergy should and should not go for their own safety and well-being. Two examples follow:

> Rev. Mia Thomas: Our male clergy colleagues can be the worst, least safe folks to be around. My first year as a pastor I had other clergywomen pull me aside to make sure I was aware of the "unofficial list" of clergymen who are not safe for women, as they are known for speaking and/or acting inappropriately (sexually, specifically) to young women, colleagues included. It was so awful to know how well known this is, and to wonder what kind of harm has not been stopped in the churches they serve. (We had a bishop who gave lip service to caring about this, but who did

---

[1] Andrea Roske-Metcalfe, "Do & Don't: An Open Letter to Older Male Senior Pastors Regarding Your Working Relationship with Younger Women/ Femme/Non-Binary* Associate Colleagues," *Fidelia Magazine,* June 5, 2018, https://youngclergywomen.org/do-dont-an-open-letter-to-older-male-senior-pastors-regarding-your-working-relationships-with-younger-women-femme-non-binary-associate-colleagues/.

[2] Ibid.

> nothing/very little when given the opportunity to actively do something about it).
>
> Rev. Evelyn Thompson: I received quiet, subtle hints on who not to be alone with, as well as male colleagues who knew their male colleagues were inappropriate and dangerous, and said, "Well, that's just John ..."

But as discussed in the first chapter, it is not only men who have created these environments for sexism to thrive. Women, especially older women clergy, can be some of the worst colleagues for younger women clergy. Some believe that if they were forced to survive these structures, then the next generation should have to as well. As Pastor Carol Martin reflected:

> I think a hard thing to be acknowledged is that some of our colleagues who are women are also not necessarily allies either, although for different reasons. At least in my neck of the woods there is a real generational divide between female clergy. It can be quite rough when it's the women holding up the toxic sexism because they worked through it and so feel we should as well.

This causes women clergy to be constantly aware of the culture around them. In many cases, they are constantly expecting sexist statements, being dismissed, or having people defer to males. Hypervigilance causes very real and very serious changes in our biology. Our bodies respond to the constant flow of cortisol in anticipation of something unwanted happening to us. Medical experts have connected these experiences of chronic stress to increased risk for anxiety, depression, headaches, sleep disorders, heart health, and more.[3] The onslaught of sexist comments and treatment by the church can have this impact on women's bodies.

This can be as ritualistic as the Sunday liturgy. Rev. Laura White shared with me about an older man in her congregation who approaches her after worship every Sunday. He says to her that she is the "prettiest priest he ever saw." Often he tries to kiss her cheek

[3] Mayo Clinic Staff, "Chronic Stress Puts Your Health at Risk," Mayo Clinic, https://www.mayoclinic.org/healthy-lifestyle/stress-management/in-depth/stress/art-20046037.

or hand while saying it. If there are others around him, he invites them to agree with him. The others present either agree or, at the very least, do not tell him this is inappropriate. The pastor said, "I pray every week that it won't happen. And then it does." Her body clenches as he approaches, fearful of the interaction about to come, and then she has to abide in the anxiety.

The frequency of these experiences causes a hypervigilance women live with every day. This stems from the way rape culture has taught women to be aware at all times. Despite the terrible fact that there is always some sexist behavior lurking behind the next corner, there is never a consideration of ways to stop it from happening. Instead, women clergy pray they will not have to deal with the next unwanted comment, the next dismissal of their authority, the next deference to their male colleague. Then they live with the pain of it happening again.

Each of these impacts—being forced to choose themselves or the church, signaling to others safe spaces, and the reality of hypervigilance—costs female clergy greatly. There is a limit to the willingness of women to engage in cultures that force this type of burden to be carried. As a result, the church continues to suffer the loss of gifted clergy who refuse to be agents of the patriarchal system, turning over them and their lives for the sake of an oppressive force.

Refusing to Ignore the Problem

Despite the efforts of patriarchy to convince them otherwise, women are noticing that something is wrong. Much like the women of second-wave feminism, the feeling of malaise is becoming hard to ignore and even harder to avoid. This is manifesting in significant changes in the livelihoods of women in all realms. A recent survey found that women are leaving leadership roles in corporate America at the highest rates ever.[4] This survey discovered that women find it important "to work for companies that prioritize career advancement, flexibility, employee well-being as well as diversity, equity and

---

[4] Morgan Smith, "'It's a Disastrous Situation': Women Leaders Are Leaving Companies at the Highest Rate Ever." *CNBC*, October 18, 2022, https://www.cnbc.com/2022/10/18/women-leaders-are-leaving-companies-at-highest-rate-ever-leanin-mckinsey-co-report.html.

inclusion."[5] If those needs continue to be unmet, women are leaving—showing loyalty to their values over their companies.

The same reality is happening in the church, with women clergy departing professional ministry at rates higher than their male counterparts'.[6] In an era when congregational survival in mainline Protestantism is often precarious and the number of people entering ministry overall is declining, the loss of women clergy at such significant rates is a point of concern for what might be next. Like their corporate colleagues, women clergy appear to be choosing the value of themselves over their work. These clergywomen are choosing themselves instead of the patriarchal structures that have tried to convince them to sacrifice everything in support of the system.

This is carrying over to women in the pews as well. Among Gen Z, women are outpacing men leaving the church. With more than 60 percent of Gen Z women identifying as feminists concerned about the treatment of women throughout society, they are becoming less likely to participate in institutions that uphold these oppressive structures.[7] This new generation has broken decades-old patterns. Women are now more likely than their male peers to disaffiliate with organized religion.

Even if clergywomen are not fully departing their roles or the church, they are living with the reality of less confidence in their call and less fulfillment from their work. A recent Barna study released in 2023 showed this trend, after surveyors repeated a survey from 2015. The 2023 survey results for women clergy were striking. The most recent data shows that 25 percent of women report that "they've lost confidence in their calling since they started ministry."[8] (This is up from 3 percent of all clergy in 2015 and compared to just 12 percent

---

[5] Ibid.

[6] "45th Anniversary of the Ordination of Women — Executive Summary Clergy Questionnaire Report 2015," ELCA.

[7] Daniel Cox and Kelsey Eyre Hammond, "Young Women Are Leaving Church in Unprecedented Numbers: The Gender Divide in Religiosity Has Flipped," Survey Center on American Life, April 4, 2024, https://www.americansurveycenter.org/newsletter/young-women-are-leaving-church-in-unprecedented-numbers/.

[8] "Excerpt: A Rapid Decline in Pastoral Security," Barna, March 15, 2023, https://www.barna.com/research/pastoral-security-confidence/.

of male clergy in 2023.[9]) This is a primary indicator of women clergy who are most at risk of leaving the church.

If, after all these years, the rates of women clergy are still remarkably low and women clergy are leaving church leadership at an increased pace, the church will soon be at a crisis point in terms of leadership. The success of the patriarchy will always be at the expense of the lives of the women it works to oppress. These conflicting points are forcing a choice for women clergy.

---

[9] Ibid.

Chapter 6

What Big Lies You Have

Patriarchy sets traps. Just like the way patriarchy convinced women that removing official barriers to ordination in the church was the end of overt sexism, patriarchy continues to morph and set pitfall after pitfall in front of the work of true liberation. It will disguise itself and stop at nothing to take what it wants, limiting the humanity of everyone involved.

My favorite fairy tale as a child was "Little Red Riding Hood." I loved the strong intuition of the main character who refused to believe what did not make sense despite the repeated attempts to convince her otherwise. It is a good message to keep in mind when we consider the lengths that sexism goes to in order to maintain power and consume anything that might challenge it. Just like the wolf in the story, patriarchy slips on a nightgown, slides under the sheets, and pulls the quilt up to its eyes—all the while trying to convince us that it is something sweet and wholesome rather than cunning and deadly.

Benevolent Patriarchy

The allure of benevolent patriarchy is an intoxicating trap. Patriarchy takes this disguise, appearing to champion women while simultaneously limiting their true involvement and leadership in the world. Benevolent patriarchy, like all forms of patriarchy, ultimately works to maintain the power structures of this world that benefit men. Many times this manipulation is to convince women that certain spaces are safer than they truly are so as to avoid any critique of their actions.

This is an additional challenge for women in denominations that have long removed official barriers and yet have continued to systematically keep women out of key leadership roles, diminished their authority, or provided them less than their male counterparts. This masking of the oppressive nature of sexism makes it all the more devious and difficult to navigate. This dynamic influences other obstacles that patriarchy has put in place.

Unfortunately, mainline Protestant denominations can be the worst perpetrators of benevolent patriarchy. After all, they can easily hide behind decades of women's right to ordination while simultaneously sweeping the statistical evidence that women's leadership is not supported under the rug. They will denounce aggressive acts against women—such as the denial of women's ordination—only to limit women's leadership in more surreptitious ways.

A public example of benevolent patriarchy played out in the religious landscape in the United States in the early summer of 2023. It is often easy to spot, as it frequently follows instances of blatant sexism—offering an initial surge in support for the oppressed women to mask the same, albeit less outwardly malicious, oppressions. When the Southern Baptist Convention met in June of 2023, they affirmed a vote, with an overwhelmingly positive response, to allow "only men as any kind of pastor or elder as qualified by Scripture." (As the vote was taken by a raised-ballot card, the official tally is unknown. However, this vote came a day after two votes to affirm expulsion of congregations in the Southern Baptist Convention that allowed women clergy to serve. Those votes were over 90 percent affirmative.)[1]

In the wake of this decision, denominations and other allies of women's ordination took to public forums—denouncing the action of the Southern Baptist Convention and espousing support for women in the church. This is often the way that patriarchy lures women into spaces that are not supporting their best interests, but rather the interests of systems that are most effective when their oppressive ways are not questioned. Benevolent patriarchy works to restore the equilibrium—keeping people from noticing the same lack of support

[1] Ruth Graham and Elizabeth Dias, "Southern Baptists Vote to Further Expand Restrictions on Women as Leaders," *New York Times*, June 14, 2023, https://www.nytimes.com/2023/06/14/us/southern-baptist-women-pastors-ouster.html.

for women that exists in these spaces, even if they do not come with overt sexism.

Reflecting on the messages she had seen on social media following the Southern Baptist Convention's decision, Rev. Shayna Jo Wible wrote a piece for *Fidelia,* the online magazine of Young Clergy Women International. In her piece she calls out the truth of benevolent patriarchy. She describes types of posts she has seen on social media that denounce the Southern Baptist Convention's vote and express support for women clergy. She is unconvinced of their sincerity. She writes, "Many of these posts are by pastors and congregations who I know to have silenced, minimized, and failed to uplift the female pastors in their midst. I, for one, have had enough of these empty claims. Support for female pastors in word or ruling is not the same as support in action."[2]

In poetic form, she continues to describe how benevolent patriarchy manifests in the church. Her words so clearly capture the way this guise of sexism is used as superficial support of women's leadership in the church. She writes, as if to a male minister:

> Supporting women who pastor doesn't mean:
>
> Inviting them to the table
> just to ignore what they say.
>
> Giving them a chance to preach
> just on the weeks the male pastor doesn't want to anyway.
>
> Acknowledging they have good ideas
> just to pass them off as your own.
>
> Promoting their presence on leadership
> just to boost your own image as forward-thinking or
> inclusive.
>
> Declaring they bring unique gifts
> while ensuring those gifts don't make the male pastors
> look lacking.

[2] Shayna Jo Wible, "Support for Women Who Pastor," *Fidelia Magazine,* June 16, 2023, https://youngclergywomen.org/support-for-women-who-pastor/.

Saying you value their femininity
to then imply it makes them weak or silly.

Championing women publicly
but then silencing the women leaders in your own church.

Calling them equal
to then always defer to men first.

Overusing them 'til they burn out
to then say maybe they just didn't have what it takes.

Posting about how great women pastors are
instead of checking in on how you treat the ones you actually know.

Making space for their voice
so long as they're saying what you already wanted to hear.

Wanting a woman as a pastor
so long as she kind of acts like a man.

Cheering them on
so long as they fit the mold of what you think women who pastor should be.

Oh yes, you support women pastors,
so long as you don't have to change the systems that were made for and by men.[3]

Recognizing benevolent patriarchy is difficult. It is tempting for women to align themselves with professed allies. It can be so alluring that women will come to ignore or accept the other oppressive behaviors that this guise of sexism enables to continue. After all, it seems like a point of respite in a world that is filled with a barrage of sexism at every turn. The more explicit oppressions in the sections that follow will show the prevalence of this benevolent patriarchy. In part, this is due to the way the examples are seated in the experiences of mainline Protestant denominations. As they claim support for women's leadership, we need to be aware of the places they continue to fall short of truly championing these women.

---

[3] Ibid.

Winning at Patriarchy

In early 2024 the world started paying attention, in a way that felt almost like the first time ever, to women's sports. More people watched the women's college basketball finals, and ticket prices were nearly double those of the men's finals. The pinnacle came when Caitlin Clark, a guard for the University of Iowa, was the first pick of the WNBA draft and officially joined the Indiana Fever. Her four-year contract totals $338,000. Her male counterpart—the number one pick in the NBA that same year, Victor Wembanyama playing for the San Antonio Spurs—would be offered a four-year contract of $55 million.[4]

To say there is a disparity between the compensation of these two athletes is an understatement. But this problem goes far beyond that. Of course, I want nothing more than for Caitlin Clark to be paid the same as a man in the same position. However, to do so means that men have set the standard. Raising her up to his level means that she has won, that she has conquered some attempt of patriarchy to limit what she is capable of and deserving of. After all, equity in a capitalistic society will always mean hierarchy.

The same is true when we examine clergy compensation. Using my own denomination as an example, women on average are paid 9 percent less than their male colleagues. (Men make 7 percent more in their first calls.)[5] But this disparity goes beyond the paycheck. In the same way that women are provided with less compensation, they are also given less authority, formally and informally. As of 2021, women clergy make up only 22 percent of the lead roles in the largest congregations in the ELCA. The same survey showed that women of color wait the longest for calls, often exceeding twenty-four months from seminary graduation to the date of their first call. While the research has not been done explicitly on the reality of queer women, anecdotally they also wait longer and receive less compensation than their straight counterparts. Very frequently, clergywomen with other marginalized identities are only offered part-time calls.

---

[4] Celeste Davis, "Is the Goal of Feminism to Win at Patriarchy?" *Matriarchal Blessing*, June 9, 2024, https://celestemdavis.substack.com/p/goal-of-feminism.

[5] "50th Anniversary Ordination of Women Survey Results," ELCA.

This is the game that patriarchy plays, making things out of alignment—especially by giving women less than what men receive. The goal, then, becomes to win, to achieve, to move out of the limitations placed before women and meet the same standard as men, regardless of the cost. This is true even when there does not seem to be real competition.

This is also the space where racism furthers the complex oppression of patriarchy. Calling back to the first-wave feminists who objected to Black men gaining the right to vote before them, we see the way white supremacy culture makes everything into a zero-sum game. Competing or trying to conquer others on some path to the top is a tactic that these oppressive structures use to stay in place and compromise the ability for anyone to be liberated. This is the echo of the colonial narrative, that we must overcome something in order to be free from something else. We need to recognize that the best path forward is a new structure, a new experience that no longer pits people against each other.

Many years ago, during college, I overheard two male pastors talking about one of their female colleagues. One said, "I heard people say that she is the best woman preacher in the ELCA"—an obvious compliment and testament to the way she was respected by the church at large. But it was what his conversation partner said that really matters. He challenged the comment made by the first pastor and replied, "Why can't we just say that she is the best preacher in the ELCA?"

These comments suggest that there was some common knowledge about the ranking of preachers in my denomination. (There is no such thing.) It also suggests that there are two different rankings—one for men and one for women. While the second pastor's challenge breaks down the second fallacy, it still shows some level of competition. (Who among the sixteen thousand-plus clergy of the ELCA is best at proclaiming the word of God?) These two (male) pastors thought they might know the answer.

All of these ways that we limit what women can achieve creates this deeply competitive environment. These obstacles are meant to convince us that there is something to overcome, something to beat—and, if we do, something that we will be rewarded or deemed some type of champion over patriarchy. But unfortunately, it is not against patriarchy that we are competing.

Part of this scam patriarchy runs is to pit women against each other. Far too often oppressive structures can convince women that we are in competition with each other. An illusion of power can be won by undermining or cutting down other women. It is a tactic of patriarchy to distract and disadvantage women. After all, if women are too busy competing with other women and compromising their success, they will not have time to recognize or combat the true enemy that sexism has created.

This issue took to the stage in *Six: The Musical,* where the six wives of King Henry VIII compete to convince the audience that their experience with the monarch was the worst. In turn, each queen presents her story through song, laying out her struggle as the most difficult—that is, until the sixth wife, Catharine Parr, refuses to participate. She challenges the other wives to name any reason, other than their relationship to their husband, that they should compete against each other. In their awakening to this truth, Anne Boleyn, wife number two, enthusiastically affirms this sentiment, saying, "Since the only thing we have in common is our husband, grouping us is an inherently comparative act and as such unnecessarily elevates a historical approach ingrained in patriarchal structures."[6]

Parr refuses to compete. Boleyn names why. The church needs women like them to echo the same message. When that happens, women are able to stand with and for other women. The togetherness of that mutuality does incredible damage to sexism. In these competitions no one wins. In fact, much is lost. Relationships, trust, and concern for others are often lost to this fallacy of competition.

Honorary Men

If patriarchy is a game and winning is the goal, then the uniform is that of men. Since men set the standards of success, they also set the standards of what it takes to get there. This is much like in the Disney movie *Mulan*, where the title character impersonates a man in

[6] Toby Marlow and Lucy Moss, *Six: The Musical,* December 18, 2017.

order to gain access to the man-only space of the military. Likewise, women are often told to change who they are to be more in-line with the male standard, role, or appearance.

This is among the most frequent "advice" given to women clergy as to how they should navigate these systems that try to limit who they are. Pastor Ann Miller shared this: "When I first got ordained, a female lay leader told me that I should keep wearing skirts and dresses so I wouldn't look like one of those women priests trying to look like a man."

Being told to avoid the trap of trying to be an honorary man is one thing; being told to be more masculine is another. Pastor Victoria Sawyer said, "A volunteer I run into at the hospital a lot when visiting congregants has sought me out on multiple occasions to tell me that he can't see me as a pastor. He says 'you need to grow a beard and grow up to be a pastor.'"

But, of course, it is not just about our appearance but also the spaces we inhabit. Another clergywoman, Pastor Jayne Ellis, is the first female pastor to serve her congregation. She gets comments about her office being "too feminine" and "not professional." Her wall of curated art—including multiple icons of Mary—is considered to be out of alignment with what this congregation has come to expect their pastor's office should look like. A personalized space, filled with beautiful representations of the divine and the faithful response of God's people, is not what their male pastors chose. In order to be seen as a pastor, like her male predecessors, she is told that she needs to conform with their design choices.

This way of thinking means that beautiful things are feminine and somehow bad or wrong. But God continues to call us all to make beautiful things that reflect the vast creative nature of God's own creative actions. The same God who paints the night sky and fills fields with flowers does not need stark white walls to define what a church office should be.

Moreover, God who made us in God's own image does not create us to fit a mold or a societal definition of gender. Those who embody what we consider feminine attributes reflect just as much who God is as those who embody masculine attributes. The vast diversity of genders reflects the deep beauty of the divine.

Joining the Oppression

One of the worst traps patriarchy sets is to embody the old adage: if you can't beat them, join them. Oppressive powers try to convince people that they are unchangeable and undefeatable. As such, after failed attempts to break apart the things that hold them back, people can easily fall into the trap of joining these oppressions. The promise of some form of privilege instead of continued oppression is beyond tempting.

In my elementary school, second-grade recess was ruled by one game: Red Rover. Standing in two lines across from each other, we would call out: "Red Rover! Red Rover! Send Ashley right over!" Of course, the goal was to keep our line intact, grabbing deftly onto arms of our neighbors while Ashley —or whomever had been summoned across the play yard_ran full speed, hoping to break the chain of her fellow classmates. Of course, if Ashley was unsuccessful, she would be forced to join the ranks of that line, working toward having all players on one side.

Far too often our work of liberation becomes a game of Red Rover. When we call for someone to try to break apart the oppressive behavior of the world, their work is met with significant resistance. And, if they are unsuccessful, they often easily find themselves in the same oppressive behavior they were trying to undo.

This trap is especially true for white women. Much like the foremothers who abandoned Black and brown women in the fight for justice, the same trap presents itself again and again. Oppressive powers force people to align themselves as closely to the center of power as possible. As straight, white men are the strongest holders of power in our society, white women will align themselves racially in order to benefit from the privileges granted to white persons. White women have been duped by white supremacy to sacrifice the needs of Black women for their own gain. They have been seduced by the promises of success and power to keep the evidence of doing so out of sight and out of mind.

Calling on my own denomination again as an example, we see the deep disparity in the length of time it took from the first white woman to be ordained to the first Black woman. We live in a time when that disparity continues to be perpetuated. But those promises of privilege are a deception. There are limits to what is gained, and the lives of the most vulnerable become further sacrificed to these systems. In the end, no one actually advances. God calls us to turn over these tables and remove the illusion of power from these oppressions. We must remember that our liberation is bound up in that of others.

Chapter 7

Mortared by Tradition

When patriarchy is not setting traps, it is building walls. The only way to truly build a feminist church is first to take down these barriers so that something new might be established. Otherwise, a truly liberating expression of the church will not be built on a firm foundation, but rather resting on unlevel and unsteady ground. The method of adding women's leadership into the church did not include adjusting the patriarchal structures on which it has been established. The success of women has been limited to their ability to survive these realities. In order to stop perpetuating this culture, we must first tear down these structures that have only served men and build a truly supportive space.

When we consider this work like renovating a home, we can focus on the goals of creating the church to be a place of comfort and belonging. But that means we do not simply add on to what we have, cementing the old under the new. If you watch any home renovation special, you know that the first step, before any work to make the new begins, is demolition. As we see in the *Fixer Upper* craze, more often than not the best way to create the space we want in the place we have is to strip it down to the studs.

This does not mean that we need to destroy the foundation or tear out load-bearing walls. Like Chip and Joanna Gaines, we must see the potential richness of the space and imagine what can be possible. In the case of this work, we need to claim that the church has "good bones." The church will remain steadfast in the faith on which it was built but free from the constraints humanity has constructed. That also means the church needs to be willing to swing a sledgehammer at the walls that have been built in places where an open-concept floor plan is far more in line with God's hopes for creation.

Patriarchy fights to keep those walls that it has built. Throughout these pages, we will look at each barrier and why we need to remove it in order to create a more sound, stable structure for the future. While the hope is for all that oppresses to tumble, there is no way to name or consider every obstacle that women encounter. But we can look at those who most directly impact women clergy, especially as has been articulated in my conversations with colleagues and my own experiences. While these experiences are not unique to women clergy, they are manifested within the church in particular ways.

When this work of dismantling is done, we can truly create something new: a place where the lives of all are called holy, the experiences of women are seen as valuable assets, and we respond with abundant equality. This is how we will embody the reign of God in this world.

A Man's World

The default setting on all structures is set to the experiences of men. Everything from physical structures to medical research to product development is designed, tested, and constructed to complement the lived experiences of men. This means that women, their bodies, their experiences, and their very lives are not considered valuable. The world quickly claims that which is male to be the norm and what all things should be created to accommodate.

One profound example of this comes from the automobile-manufacturing world. A 2021 report revealed that there has never been an automobile crash study done with a crash dummy that represents an average woman. The crash dummies that are supposed to represent women are four-foot-eleven and 108 pounds, where the average height and weight of women in the United States is five-foot-four and 170 pounds. The body structure of the smaller dummy is also based on a male body type in proportions. More striking, though, the same study found that most crash tests do not put a female dummy in the driver's seat.[1] Yes, the assumption of those testing the safety

[1] Sophie Putka, "Why Are There No Crash Test Dummies that Represent Average Women?," *Discover Magazine,* February 16, 2021, https://www.discovermagazine.com/technology/why-are-there-no-crash-test-dummies-that-represent-average-women.

features on cars is that women are never in the driver's seat of the vehicle. If the working assumption of the safety industry is that women do not drive vehicles, then it is not a far stretch when the experiences of women are not considered in other spaces where they could be in control. (In 2025 this issue finally made it to the federal level, with the Department of Transportation announcing an updated requirement for car companies to test using a test dummy that more accurately represents the anatomy of women. However, the testing using this dummy is not expected until 2027 or 2028.[2])

When women leaders are in spaces that are not built for them and they do not succeed, they are criticized. This happens even when the spaces are quite literally unsafe because they have not been constructed with consideration of the lives of women. Yet women are still expected to use these structures. After all, there is no expectation that women would not drive a car. There has just become, through society's patriarchal bent, the concession that women would drive a car that might not be safe for them to do so. The lives of women are worth less than changes to the industry to test safety in a way that is representative of the whole population.

One way this has manifested in churches is through microphones. Here again the equipment does not match the needs of the women using them, and the outcome is women being criticized for who they are. Women clergy have been told over and over that they need to change the pitch or tone of their voice because they cannot be heard (or told to wear lipstick so that people can hear them better). Many women clergy shared this specific experience with me as something told to them repeatedly of how to "improve" themselves. Two women shared these experiences:

> Rev. Emily King: As a part of my ordination process, the personnel team at the local church was invited to give feedback to me and our [denomination's judicatory]. They made an official recommendation for my file saying that I needed to pursue voice lessons to "alter the pitch of your

[2] Julie Tsirkin and Emma Dion, "Federal Government to Require Car Companies to Use Female Crash Test Dummies," *NBC News*, November 20, 2025, https://www.nbcnews.com/politics/politics-news/dot-female-crash-test-dummy-regulation-rcna244949.

voice" so that it would be more pleasant and lower for preaching.

Rev. Nora Robinson: A supervisor for field education told me to lower the pitch of my voice, in other words, to make it sound more masculine, because my soprano voice didn't sound confident or like a preacher. People wouldn't be able to listen to me.

This issue has nothing to do with the "pitch" of a woman's voice, but rather the frequency of women's voices and the challenge for higher-frequency voices to be made louder through technology. Microphones have long been created to amplify lower-frequency voices, typically a distinguishing characteristic of men's voices.[3] When women clergy speak into microphones in churches, they are using technology designed to keep their voices from being heard well.

Perhaps clergy-wear is even more illustrative. Until very recently, most companies selling women's clergy shirts made them in ways that represented a very narrow and very distinct taste in women's clothing. In addition to the standard black, women's shirts only came in pastels—hues of baby pink, lavender, and mint green—in contrast to men's shirts that came in black, gray, navy, and, of course, the deep purple reserved for bishops in many denominations. These darker colors have been traditionally associated with professionalism, unlike the Easter egg pastels of women's shirts. The mass production of women's shirts in these colors seems to suggest that these colors, which might be described as "delicate" or "ladylike," are what women clergy would prefer to wear. Furthermore, the way women's clergy shirts were constructed made them shapeless and in stiff fabrics. In other words, these shirts were made in the same way that men's shirts were made. The primary difference is that women's shirts did not include breast pockets. Shirts made this way do not provide necessary accommodations to the curves and shapes of women's bodies (not to mention a primary company selling clergy shirts is named "Friar Tuck," logoed with a tonsured monk in a brown habit, which is not a

[3] Tina Tallon, "A Century of 'Shrill': How Bias in Technology Has Hurt Women's Voices," *The New Yorker,* September 3, 2019, https://www.newyorker.com/culture/cultural-comment/a-century-of-shrill-how-bias-in-technology-has-hurt-womens-voices.

brand name or image that exudes confidence in understanding how to best dress women's bodies).

When we operate with these assumptions—men drive cars, men use microphones, men wear clerics—it is unsurprising that the female experience is not represented and, as a result, criticized for not being adequate. When the church goes a step further in using exclusively male language for God, we come to a point where God's default is also male. The words we use to talk about God reveal what we believe to be true about God. If we only use words associated with one gender, then we reflect that gender back on God. The reverse is also true, positing that the image of God reflected in humanity is male.

This is dangerous theology. It others the bodies and experiences of women as being far from the holiness and sacredness of what God has made and called good. When this is the church's operating assumption, it leads easily and quickly to women being treated in ways that are less than their male counterparts. It perpetuates a divide between males who represent this perceived theological truth and the women who do not. It provides a distorted justification for the ways women receive less despite having to operate in a world that is not built for them.

Many exude this theology to exclude women outright from ordination. When we embody the same beliefs in denominations where women are allowed to be ordained, we still keep women from truly living out their vocation. While we can look at microphones and clergy-wear as things that can change—and there are companies working to advance these products for a more diverse consumer base—there are other things that seemingly cannot change.

When the first female pastor came to my congregation while I was in the sixth grade, she was far shorter than the male colleagues who preceded her or worked with her. The pulpit had been built for a person whose height was representative of the average height of a man. Her father built her a wooden box with a handle that she could carry into the pulpit to adjust her height. She had to create and take with her a way to change who she was in order to fit the space that had not been designed for her and would be difficult to change in a historic sanctuary. This is just another example of how the world is made for men and the burden to fit into those spaces is always placed on women. This creates an unfair and untenable situation for women.

But it can go further, into sexist requests for male leadership. As I mentioned earlier, a female pastor at my church was asked not to officiate a wedding as it would "ruin the photos." I lived through a similar encounter. Once I had a conversation with some non-members looking for an officiant. They were interested in a religious service, but the pastor of the church the bride grew up in would not officiate the service because she was living with her fiancé. She went on to ask me if my male colleague was available to officiate the service because they wanted a male pastor. This was despite the fact that a male pastor, and the values of his congregation, were causing this search for an officiant in the first place. I told her that my male colleague was not available (he would never have agreed to do this wedding knowing the reason for her request of his leadership) but that I would be happy to do the service if they chose. I never heard back from them.

Pastor Jade Williams shared this story with me: She was out of town when she got a call to officiate a funeral. She called a (male) colleague to arrange for coverage. He told her that "the family would prefer anyone with a penis." In this claim the genitalia of the person presiding was more important than the leadership they would provide. In all of these cases, the embodiment of a male leader is valued high above any skills women have to offer.

Unlevel Playing Field

Women do not receive equal access, compensation, assumption of authority, accolade, or support in all areas of their lives. This disparity is part of what makes it so difficult to remove the barriers that the patriarchy has so well constructed. Paying women less keeps their power in check. Making sure they are unable to obtain lead roles holds their secondary place firm. The patriarchy will do anything to make sure that men are always higher, always more compensated, always more accomplished than women.

Sometimes this work of oppressive structures is put on display in an embodied way. In 2017, after a 4–2 victory over the Colorado Rockies, Los Angeles Dodgers outfielder Kiké Hernandez decided to stand on a bucket for his postgame interview with Dodgers reporter Kelli Tennant.[4] Tennant is exceptionally tall, listed as six foot two, and, of course, was also wearing heels on the sidelines. Hernández only measures five foot eleven in comparison, and was wearing cleats. By standing on the bucket, Hernández made himself taller than the female reporter who was interviewing him. Many (male) sports analysts called this nothing more than one of Hernández's "pranks" that he is known to do. Regardless of the intention, the message was the same: Hernández did not want to appear below a woman in any way. This is a very tangible embodiment of the way women lose any perceived advantage they might have in the world.

Of course, the reality and the disparities are far beyond this one postgame moment. According to the 2025 World Economic Forum, it will take 123 years to close the gender gap, at the current pace of societal change.[5] (The gender gap is a measurement of equality across the economy, politics, health, and education.[6]) In other words, no woman currently alive will live to see the gender gap closed. This reality is still a dream, many generations yet to come, held precariously on the presumption that changes in society continue at this glacially positive trajectory.

This does not mean that women are less competent in their positions. In fact, the opposite is true. Despite receiving less compensation, women have to prove a higher competency or proficiency than might be required of men. An example I heard once was the contrast between Ginger Rogers and Fred Astaire. As a woman in the dance world, Ginger had to be able to dance backwards in heels but would receive less recognition and compensation than Fred Astaire. The same is true in every field. Women are expected to accomplish something beyond what would be expected of men and receive fewer accolades or less compensation.

---

[4] Erik Chesterton, "Kiké Hernandez Decided to Stand on a Bucket for His Postgame Interview," *MLB*, April 20, 2017, https://www.mlb.com/cut4/dodgers-kike-hernandez-stood-on-a-bucket-in-his-postgame-interview-c225429262.

[5] "Global Gender Gap Report 2025," World Economic Forum, June 11, 2025, https://www.weforum.org/publications/global-gender-gap-report-2025/in-full/benchmarking-gender-gaps-2025/#:~:text=Among%20the%20145%20economies%20included%20in%20both%20the%202024%20and,of%20around%200.1%20percentage%20points.

[6] Ibid.

Like previously shared, women clergy are frequently assumed not to be the pastor. But even more illustrative of this is that people will defer to a man whenever he is in the space, whether or not he is the one with formal authority. A social media post went viral in 2023 showcasing this reality in an interesting way. The post read: "A friend's male assistant is a fake email account she runs because people called her 'difficult' and 'impossible' for having small windows of availability until 'he' started running interference and then people just accepted she was ... busy."[7] In this case, people showed deference to the authority of a man who was not even real. The illusion of absolute authority is such that it can and will be given to a man who does not exist. It is telling what is believed or not based on the source and the assumed authority.

When women's lives are dismissed in these ways, women are pushed aside and sometimes not even considered. While I was in my final year of seminary, my father was asked to serve on the call committee of my home congregation for an open associate pastor position. The president of the church council approached my dad one Sunday after worship to talk about the process. The president was a man, two years younger than me. During their conversation he asked if my dad agreed with others—that they should consider only male candidates. My dad was shocked at this statement; it was the first he was hearing this. He asked the president if he knew what I was currently completing my schooling to do. (This was a purely rhetorical question. Of course the president knew what I was doing; we had grown up together in the congregation. It is also important to note that, because this was my home congregation, I would not have been considered for the position regardless of my gender.) My dad decided he could not serve in a call committee that was supporting this thinking and stepped down from that position. The call process resulted in a male candidate being called to that position.

In this scenario, there was some consensus among at least a group in the congregation that it would not even be worthwhile to

---

[7] Bess Kalb, "A friend's male assistant is an email account she runs because people called her 'difficult' and 'impossible' for having small windows of availability until 'he' started running interference and then people just accepted she was —— busy. I AM VERY INTO THIS,"" X, July 29, 2020, https://twitter.com/bessbell/status/1288491459344138243?lang=en.

consider a female candidate. There were likely a number of reasons or justifications attached to their thinking: the last two associates had been female and had not stayed long, the senior pastor was getting closer to retirement and this associate could be an internal candidate (and the heir apparent would obviously have to be male), or they simply did not want a woman in a leadership position. Whatever the reason, the assumption that even my father would agree to consider only male candidates was real. There was also belief that there would be assent to this thinking, even from someone who was the father of a clergywoman.

While I do not know the particular reaction to my father stepping down from the committee, a common set of responses occur when this type of thinking is challenged. When called out on this oppressive behavior, there is often both defensiveness and disbelief. Of course no one wants to be considered sexist, so they push back when confronted with evidence that they are working against women. However, when women are told that their experiences are simply not true or at least exaggerated, we encounter an even greater obstacle to a liberated future.

Disbelief

One of the greatest obstacles in the church is disbelief. This is not in reference to any doubts of faith, but rather doubting the legitimacy of claims of sexist oppression. Frequently women are told that their experiences could not have truly happened or that they are fabricating the details. This is in part because if these stories are true it means that many would have to reevaluate everything they believe to be true about the church. Men would have to confront the sexism that they benefit from and that oppresses others. They would have to name the truth of what patriarchy has done and continues to do to the lives of women. They would have to risk losing the power that is awarded to them by virtue of their gender. It is far easier to exist in a state of denial, ignorance, and disbelief.

One way to see this disbelief is when men are confronted with the information provided by women about their experiences. The men will exhibit discomfort and challenge the validity of the claims.

Sometimes the men who encounter these situations will attempt to label the experience as an outlier—a one-off comment made by someone who does not know better—or discredit the source of the information. This is the explanation they give rather than naming it for what it truly is: a symptom of the patriarchy.

In 2018 the North Carolina synod of the ELCA created a video that was shared widely among clergy groups.[8] To create the video, the synod contacted women clergy serving in the state and asked them to report sexist statements that had been said to them. Here are some of the comments used in the video:

- "You're the first woman preacher I've ever met. Are they all as good looking as you?"
- "I've never met a female pastor before. What do I call you? Pastorette?"
- "You're like a little girl playing pastor up there."
- "We called you because we knew we could afford you. Women pastors are cheaper."
- "You should just be grateful you're getting a call at all as a female."

The synod then recruited male pastors to read the statements in front of a camera. The men had not seen the material before filming started. As the video plays, you see the men become increasingly uncomfortable as they see and say the statements for the first time. The cameras stay rolling and capture their reactions between the read statements. They include these comments:

- "These are serious?"
- "Why would this ever come out of anyone's mouth?"
- "How is that at all appropriate?"
- "This is awkward. I don't know what type of reaction I should be giving."
- "Yuck!"

[8] North Carolina Synod (ELCA), "'Seriously?' Women in Ministry Video," October 10, 2018, YouTube, https://www.youtube.com/watch?v=bTcaAkG86QQ.

- "I'm sorry, guys. That is bullshit. That really sucks. That's uncomfortable."
- "I got through ten and I thought, 'Are we done yet?' It felt like I did twenty when I got through ten."

Presumably, the synod asked these particular men to participate in this project because they supported exposing some of the blatant sexism that their female colleagues frequently encounter. Yet it was clear from their reactions that they had no idea how dire the situation truly is, and their discomfort and disbelief was recorded. Even the video title supported the disbelief of this reality. By calling the video "Seriously?" there is a way in which every statement included from the women clergy was questioned. Did this really happen? Did this happen the way you claim it did? Did you exaggerate any of the details? Is this serious?

Acknowledging the reality, pervasiveness, and harm that sexism causes in this world is optional for men. It is not optional for women. This video puts that on full display while challenging the authenticity of the claims the women are making. One moment in this video truly highlights this challenge. The comment from the female pastor is read aloud: "You are perfect for us, except for the problem that you are a woman." After a pause, the male pastor reading it said, "I've heard that, but the other way around—when someone said, 'We're so glad that you're a man.' I said, 'Me too, but I don't know what that means.' But I did know what that means."

By telling the person who made this comment that he did not know what they meant, this pastor demonstrated the way this issue is optional for men. He claims he knew what their comment meant in a larger context. But instead of countering what they said, he affirms that he is also glad that he is a man and feigns ignorance to the larger point that person is trying to make. He enables the oppression to perpetuate and is complicit through his act of disregard (even if he did publicly apologize for understanding what his disregard perpetuated).

This challenge of disbelief is not only limited to comments made or actions against women—things that could be classified as "she said." Rather, this continues even when numeric data showcasing the problem of the ways women are treated as less than men are presented.

Despite the ways in which mathematical proof should prove more difficult to debunk, men will consistently claim the information as false or incorrectly collected, processed, or presented.

Rev. Susan Green shared a story about attending an anti-sexism training put on by her denomination's judicatory. During the day statistical data regarding clergy salaries and positions were shared. This information came directly from the denomination's national office, based on what had been reported from the congregations across the country. Unsurprisingly, it showed a large discrepancy in the pay between male and female clergy and the identities of those in the top positions in the church. One man in the room claimed that this information could not be correct and debated the validity of the data so significantly it impacted the training.

If the information presented is correct (which it is), it means that these men need to confront the privileges they are afforded for no reason other than their gender. If they do that, they must recognize that there is a risk of what they might lose in order to find equality. It is far easier to ignore these truths, disbelieve the evidence, and claim that the information is where the true error exists.

The path forward includes removing these obstacles so that women can flourish in the places they are called to be. This means valuing and using the experiences of women in constructing the world around us, closing the gaps in compensation and acknowledgement of success, and believing women when they say they are being treated in these oppressive ways. These structures continue to keep women in the places that least disturb the patriarchy, preserving the system that oppresses them, and to accept women's sacrifices of success and well-being as necessary costs.

The work we need to do together to liberate women from these structures involves dismantling them—taking them apart, one by one. We need to name the truth that they exist, acknowledge the pain they have caused, and make sure that they do not come back as soon as we think the work is done. The patriarchy will always seek to right itself, reestablish itself, and grow back in more callous and stronger ways, making it a constant, insidious game of whack-a-mole.

Chapter 8

Beyond the Stained Glass Ceiling

May young girls playing in the pews at worship hear a voice that sounds like theirs, in a language that is theirs, in a church that is theirs. —Nadia Bolz-Weber[1]

A feminist church is the hope of all that this book has explored. For me, that is a place where diversity and equality are so intimately intermingled that we live in the beautiful space they create together. That looks like a church that values relationship over hierarchy, truth over deceit, and justice over gain. It is a place where all marginalized people find their experiences centered and celebrated. This means employing gender justice in our lives as a way to be in relation with each other beyond what patriarchy has convinced us is possible. When women and all who are oppressed by these structures are liberated, we can start to live in the way we are called to embody—to live as this church would be to bring forth the reign of God more fully into this world.

But this is a challenging task. When we acknowledge the brokenness of what has been, we can find ourselves in a place of despair. But we do not need to remain disheartened. When we look to where God is calling the church, we see something different. We see God's work on earth as it is in heaven, where we are cherished for the way we have been made and held in a place where we are fully known. This is the place a feminist church lives and where we are called to be. Of course, to get to this place we have to work together and dream of what might be. Without wild imagination, we will enable the patriarchy to dictate what is possible. The patriarchy wants as little

[1] Nadia Bolz-Weber, "Vox Femina," *The Corners,* March 12, 2023, https://thecorners.substack.com/p/vox-femina#:~:text=May%20young%20girls%20playing%20in,grow%20to%20lead%20us%20all.

liberation as possible. Dreaming is one way to subvert that power. As Gloria Steinem famously said, "Without leaps of imagination, or dreaming, we lose the excitement of possibilities. Dreaming, after all, is a form of planning."[2]

I invited the members of Young Clergy Women International to share their hopes and dreams of a feminist church. I asked those I interviewed about their experiences of being told how to navigate around the structures of the church and what a different church might look like. I asked what it would mean for women clergy to thrive in their positions instead of trying simply to survive. I invited them to dream with me. Their answers have provided the foundation for what follows.

Each section ahead will name an attribute of a feminist church. There are, of course, other attributes that might be ascribed to such a definition. These specific characteristics are ones that presented as recurring themes within my conversations with other women clergy and ones that represent what it means to live into a space where the values of fourth-wave feminism can be realized. Together we can look at how we might build a church centered on the gospel that champions God's beloved. Only then can we live out what God has always desired for God's people. This is our deepest calling as those who have been claimed by God's love, and this is where we come to most experience that grace poured out for us that has no end.

To Tell the Truth

A feminist church will tell the truth. Honesty about the state of our humanity and the ills of patriarchy is where we need to begin. This truth-telling breaks through alternate versions of our experience and focuses on the lived reality of those on the losing side of sexism. When we do this, the distortions of facts that have been perpetuated by oppressions fall away and we can begin anew. This also means that we must believe those who speak the truth of their experiences and empower them to share their stories for the sake of healing our broken relationships. This is the essential work

---

[2] Gloria Steinem, "News," *Gloria Steinem,* http://www.gloriasteinem.com/news#:~:text=%22Without%20leaps%20of%20imagination%2C%20or,is%20a%20form%20of%20planning.%22.

that provides the foundation for all that can be built in a church that respects all people.

This is where the lives of women have been most compromised. Far too often, women have been told to keep quiet about their experiences. Speaking about sexism most unsettles the world that patriarchy has carefully constructed. After all, the power of these oppressions is most firmly held when they are not discussed, not acknowledged. When we speak the truth of patriarchy into the world, we too destroy the hold it has over us. We break the agreement it has for us to obey its absurd demands on women.

This often makes me think of the story "Rumpelstiltskin." In this German fairy tale, the queen needs to discover the name of the man who will otherwise take her firstborn child. When she is successful, speaking his name not only breaks their original agreement but drives him into the ground. The truth breaks the power he has over her and fully destroys him.

This is what it means to speak the truth of patriarchy in our world. It breaks the hold it has over us and enables us to move forward in new ways. It enables us to speak of our brokenness and the ways we have been complicit in these oppressions, the harm we have watched it perpetuate, and the silence we have kept as an act of protecting it.

Our truth-telling is a confession. It is our acknowledgement of how these structures have kept us from the relationship God desires for us with each other. It enables us to recognize where we too have participated in these oppressive powers over and against our neighbors. But in the naming of our falling short is where we are called to start anew. It is then that the liberation of forgiveness releases us to do this work for the benefit of all people.

This is why we must begin here. In telling the truth, we can start to truly do the work we are called to do for the sake of others and this world we live in. It empowers us for everything else that will follow. Truth becomes our greatest tool in breaking down the oppressive structures that have been built and laying the groundwork for all that will follow. This is how we approach the seemingly unmovable oppressions in front of us. Our words have power, and to speak the truth is the greatest act of resistance we can employ as we begin our journey to this place of wholeness.

The necessary companion of truth is belief. When women bravely tell the stories of their experiences, the ways oppressions have washed over them and pushed them back, we must believe them. We must trust that they are telling the truth. Only then can we truly embrace the gift of truth in this process. Only then can we come alongside those who have lived these experiences and respect their telling of what they know to be true.

The church needs to embody this in ways that celebrate the truth-tellers and the silence breakers, just as other parts of our world are starting to do. In 2017, "The Silence Breakers" were named the *Time* Person of the Year. The front cover of that special edition showed women who had refused to remain silent—Ashley Judd, Susan Fowler, Adama Iwu, Taylor Swift, and Isabel Pascual.[3] Each of them, along with countless others, "unleashed one of the highest-velocity shifts in our culture since the 1960s."[4] In the review of why *Time* selected them, Edward Felsenthan, editor-in-chief, wrote: "For giving voice to open secrets, for moving whisper networks onto social networks, for pushing us all to stop accepting the unacceptable, the Silence Breakers are the 2017 Person of the Year."[5] These are the same characteristics that the church should look to show forth in all aspects of our shared life.

The potential ridicule of truth-telling is a heartbreaking cost of sexism. Women who speak out sometimes face accusations of falsifying allegations and disclosing stories as a way of simply seeking revenge. There is a constant barrage of skepticism, dismissal, and invalidation of the stories that are told. This is why believing those who tell their stories is so vital. The safety of women in all parts of their lives—physical, emotional, spiritual—is on the line. We need to recognize the situation as that important and celebrate those who refuse to accept anything less. We should focus on the truth of those who speak it and elevate that action as a hallmark of a feminist church.

---

[3] Edward Felsenthal, "The Choice: Time's Editor-In-Chief on Why the Silence Breakers are the Person of the Year," *Time*, https://time.com/time-person-of-the-year-2017-silence-breakers-choice/.

[4] Ibid.

[5] Ibid.

If we are unwilling and unable to discuss the truth of what sexism has done to the lives of women, we cannot move forward. Telling the truth about this reality is imperative. When we do, when the truth is named and honored, healing and reparations are possible. The church as a whole ought to stand in solidarity with the marginalized and work robustly toward liberation. The future of the church is being shaped today and the possibility of liberation is real, but the work needs to be done. That is both an individual and a collective task.

Accompanying Allies

A feminist church will have allies in this work. Women will no longer be burdened with the responsibility of navigating the obstacles put before them on their own. Men will step up and advocate for the women in the church who are gifted and called for this work right alongside them. Men will recognize the privileges they have been granted simply because of their gender and will unquestioningly risk losing that privilege. Women will be liberated from being set against others and will be able to come alongside those who are still in oppressive settings, sharing in the freedom we are called to live in together.

Men present the greatest obstacle and the greatest potential for allies because of the way they are so fully steeped in the privileges afforded to them by their gender. Yet, in a feminist church, men will recognize that patriarchy is dangerous and detrimental to all of God's people as one of the ways our humanity's brokenness shows through in our relationships with others. Patriarchy fans the flames of toxic masculinity, teaching men that they have to conform to certain standards of what it means to be a man. This toxicity comes at the expense of men just as much as anyone.

When men are released from this bondage to oppressive structures, they are free to be the most powerful allies in this work. As the ones closest to the power center, they have a unique position to break down the barriers that keep women away from that space. In this way, men can redefine masculinity through a feminist lens—in a way that demands the same rights and privileges to be granted to their female counterparts, for the betterment of all people.

In the church, the men who have received the authority of the most privileged roles must especially be alongside women clergy in this work. Laura Stephens-Reed, a pastor and clergy coach, authored a blog post on this topic, titled "Ways Male Senior Pastors Can be Great Allies for Their Clergywomen Colleagues." While she cites many tangibles, her main point is the most important. She writes, "If I had to boil this all down, I'd simply say, 'Normalize women in leadership and share your power.'"[6]

I was lucky to have had a male colleague who was this type of ally. He normalized my leadership by respecting the boundaries of the ministry areas that were my responsibility and frequently sharing with the congregation how we worked collaboratively. He shared his power by giving us equal titles and ensuring that our public-facing ministry was equivalent, from preaching to baptizing to funerals. These simple, intentional actions make an extraordinary difference, and they must be the standard in a feminist church for working relationships between clergy regardless of gender.

This also means we must foster spaces where women are able to gather, share their experiences, affirm, and bless each other. There is something only possible when this is lived and experienced. Because of the current limitations of patriarchy in our shared life, to experience this often means creating a para-church space. One example that I know well and have shared about frequently is Young Clergy Women International. My participation in YCWI has been one of the most life-giving spaces in my life and ministry. In a place that centers the experiences of women clergy, there is a freedom from the patriarchal structures that other spaces do not have the ability to offer. YCWI has become a safe haven and sacred space for more than 2,500 clergywomen worldwide over the past two decades.

YCWI started in 2006, when a few young women clergy attending a summer conference realized they were the only ones who

---

[6] Laura Stephens-Reed, "Ways Male Senior Pastors Can Be Great Allies for Their Clergywomen Colleagues," April 25, 2023, https://www.laurastephensreed.com/blog/ways-male-senior-pastors-can-be-great-allies-for-their-clergywomen-colleagues?fbclid=IwAR1YJ4Dm_8ecPJrULVwT9IY6QBUxVMI9rbA_LLjvgdHfRkAi45kFY_4N_zU.

looked like them in the sea of their older, mostly male colleagues.[7] That reality called them to create an intentional relationship space. They recognized the need for and benefit of collegiality and comradeship among others who knew what it meant to be a young clergywoman in ministry—something that can only be fully understood by others who live it. The initial tagline of the organization reflected that truth: "You're not the only one." YCWI was rooted in this commitment to allied work, celebrated relationships, and embodied fellowship. The organization continues to live out this commitment, to the benefit of the whole church. When women clergy are strengthened and emboldened to be their full selves and respond to the way God is calling them, the church is able to embody an abundance of the life God desires for us.

When we are free from the oppressive structures that turn us against each other, we can live for each other. The church needs to be a home of and for relationships and to resist any form of domination and colonizing of women's lives with patriarchal power. A church that functions with just love at its core manifests God's grace and enables all people's thriving. Instead of channeling an assumption of scarcity, the church needs to embody the good news of the reign of God, where abundant life is possible.

Celebrating Abundance

A feminist church will operate from a place of abundance. Patriarchy tries to frighten the world into a scarcity mindset. When there is a belief that there is only so much to go around, those who are marginalized will always receive less. When we recognize that fallacy, we are free to live into the abundant life that God calls us to have. This also means letting women know that they are enough and that their success is not tied to unattainable achievements. When we do this, we can recognize a depth of giftedness that is otherwise hidden by patriarchy.

Living in abundance includes a number of tangibles, particularly in the ways that women are compensated. No longer will women

---

[7] "About Us," Young Clergy Women International, https://youngclergywomen.org/about/.

receive a percentage of the pay of their male colleagues. No longer will women have to wait longer for calls or settle for positions their giftedness does not match. No longer will anyone be told that parental leave is too expensive to fund. Instead, a feminist church will give and share abundantly as a reflection of all that we have received. In valuing the lives, experiences, and personhood of women, we will respond with the same level of respect for all people.

This is particularly difficult in a capitalistic culture. The evidence of that is easy to see. I was still in college when, at a seminary discernment event, I heard a female pastor in her first years of ministry share the story of the moment she discovered she was a "punishment" for her congregation. They had agreed to call her only because they could afford her. They adamantly opposed having a woman as a pastor. But a single woman right out of seminary matched their financial reality. As she recalled the phone call with a disgruntled member who let her in on the congregation's secret, everything came into perspective for her. All of the ways she had been treated and expected to act came from the congregation's belief that this was all they could have. There was no celebration of her gifts, just disappointment seated in scarcity.

When we were in the call process for my current colleague, who is also a woman, more than one person publicly asked: "Can we have two women pastors?" Reflecting on that question, it is hard not to call to mind the question posed to Ruth Bader Ginsburg of when there would be enough women on the Supreme Court. When she said nine, meaning every seat would be filled by a woman, she admitted that people were shocked. Yet, as she pointed out, no one ever questioned when all nine seats were filled by men.[8] So we too pointed out when asked that question that it would not be posed if both pastors were male. Having two women as pastors was not a punishment of scarcity, but rather the abundance of having clergy whose giftedness matched the congregation.

A feminist church will offer a different way of being and the ability to lean into the abundance of the gifts that we have been given.

---

[8] "Ruth Bader Ginsburg in Pictures and Her Own Words," *BBC*, September 19, 2020, https://www.bbc.com/news/world-us-canada-54218139.

This is deeply rooted in relationships that bear one another and share the power with which we have been entrusted. These examples lift up a moment of what might be at all times.

When Kyndall Rae Rothaus started dreaming up what would become an annual preaching conference that elevated women preachers, she had five weeks, no venue, no speakers, and no budget. Despite all of these things that seemed lacking, the conference became an instant national success, with the stirring title "Nevertheless She Preached." In Rothaus' own words:

> The conference was a huge success, and I was utterly blown away by what felt like a real-life miracle—all these powerful women sharing space and a platform together. Surrounded by women at the conference, I realized that the patriarchy had been keeping us from one another in all kinds of ways and with all kinds of lies and with all sorts of competitiveness, as if we had to beat one another out for the limited number of spaces available to us. But when we created our own space, there was room for everybody, and everybody had a voice, and as a result, the Holy Spirit was set loose.[9]

When Jesus says that he has come so that we might have life abundant, it means living in a place where we recognize there is more than enough. In that time and space, nothing needs to be hoarded and everything can be shared. This is the vision we need to develop and experience practically. When we live in this place of abundance, women will know that they are enough. This moves beyond any understanding that people, especially women, have to achieve some elusive standard of perfection. Instead, this enables women to know that who they are is already enough. That message is consistently held away from women, forcing them to attempt this lifelong struggle of conforming to others' unachievable expectations. But when it is spoken, so much becomes possible.

Greta Gerwig made history in the summer of 2023 by surpassing any records previously held at the box office by women directors. Gerwig both wrote and directed *Barbie.* In post-production there

---

[9] Kyndall Rae Rothaus, *Thy Queendom Come: Breaking Free from the Patriarchy to Save Your Soul,* (Minneapolis: Broadleaf Books, 2021), 70–71.

were conversations about which scenes would need to be cut for time, as is always part of the filmmaking process. One scene in particular came on the chopping block, as it did little to advance the plot. In that scene, Barbie sits at a bus stop and notices a nonagenarian sitting next to her. She looks at the older woman and says, "You're so beautiful," to which the older woman replies, "I know it!" Barbie appears moved and comforted by this older woman's example of true beauty.

In an interview, Gerwig stated that if she were to have let this scene be cut, she would not know why she was making this movie in the first place. In fact, Gerwig sees this as a holy moment, about so much more than Barbie. She explains, "The idea of a loving God who's a mother, a grandmother—who looks at you and says, 'Honey, you're doing OK'—is something I feel like I need and I wanted to give to other people."[10]

If a director can hold that hoped-for experience for a movie, so should we hold it for the church. Holding to the sacred knowledge of being enough is an offering of liberation to all who are striving toward the unattainable set up by the patriarchy. When competition is removed, anything is possible. When we know that we are enough, we find that it is more than enough, that is life abundant. It is then that we can start to see ourselves in all places that God is calling us to be.

Representation Matters

A feminist church will represent the body of Christ in all spaces. When women are excluded from spaces that they are called to inhabit, we lose a piece of the true diversity reflected in our humanity. Even if women are permitted to have official leadership positions in the church, when systemic sexism inhibits their ability to live as they have been called, the church misses out on the giftedness of so many. When we create something different people will notice, they will start to recognize themselves in those spaces and they will be reassured that God knows and sees the fullness of who they are.

I asked Pastor Kelly Wright what a feminist church would look like to her. She smiled when she thought of a church where women

---

[10] Willa Paskin, "Greta Gerwig's 'Barbie' Dream Job," *The New York Times Magazine*, July 17, 2023, https://www.nytimes.com/2023/07/11/magazine/greta-gerwig-barbie.html.

were found and seen in every type of leadership and role. "But," she said, with hesitation while her smile faded, "it would mean more women would have to be sacrificed to this system in order for more women to be represented." To her—and she is not alone in this—the only way for women to be fully represented is for enough women to "survive" until there appears to be a critical mass. Only then will there be hope that the place of women in leadership is so normalized that it goes unquestioned and unchallenged. The church needs to intentionally embody this representation in ways that support women and not base success on those who have reached a certain level of survival.

I was in sixth grade when my congregation called the first woman to be a pastor. I grew up in a historic congregation, almost two hundred years old, with an equally long history of having multiple clergy on staff. Yet it was nearly thirty years after women could be ordained in the Lutheran church in the United States that a woman came to be one of the pastors at my church. It was the first time someone who looked like me was in the pulpit and behind the altar. When she preached at my own ordination, the importance of that representation came full circle.

While I have a personal experience of the importance of a female pastor at my congregation, the representation of women in church leadership is more important than we might originally have guessed. Recent research has shown that when women have women clergy, they have higher self-esteem.[11]

Through a nationwide survey, Benjamin Knoll and Cammie Jo Bolin uncovered this connection by asking respondents about the gender of the religious leader they had growing up. But they feel the importance goes even further than the individual. Through their research they argue that the representation of women in churches is a key for the empowerment and advancement in all spheres. They state:

> To us, this strongly suggests that the rarity of female clergy in America's places of worship is at least partially to blame for the contemporary gender gap in American society.

[11] Benjamin R. Knoll and Cammie Jo Bolin, "It's Good for Girls to Have Clergywomen, Study Shows," *Religion News*, July 17, 2018, https://religionnews.com/2018/07/17/its-good-for-girls-to-have-clergywomen-study-shows/.

> Increasing the proportion of women in America's pulpits would not only improve women's psychological well-being, but would also likely help the gender gap in the workplace and other positions of societal leadership.[12]

The representation in the pulpit, they argue, is directly related to the representation of women in other places. After all, if women do not see themselves in one space, it becomes easy to notice their absence in other forums and to assume they are not meant to be there. This further shows us the way the church reaches past itself in all ways. That is why a large part of why representation matters are related to the women in the pews, everyone from the young girls to the mature grandmothers. This is how women clergy empower the women who join us in prayer and praise.

When we consider this from the perspective of empowering and equipping young girls for a future in the world and the church, we can see the support of women clergy as a way to build our shared future. Pastor Jennifer Quincy had taken her teenage daughter to a denominational gathering. As they were leaving at the end of the multi-day event, her daughter told her that she was looking forward to attending again next year. Her daughter said that what was happening in the wider church was interesting. But, more importantly, she was excited because she had an aunt and a friend who were both bishops. These two women, who had been elected to these positions of leadership, showed this teenage girl that there is a place in the church for her too.

A family with two young girls in my congregation once told me that they chose to join because our clergy team had multiple women. It was moving and humbling. This family wanted their daughters, just as my parents had, to know there was no limit on the things they could do in this world—that God could call them to any vocation, including ministry. This message is especially vital considering the cacophony of voices in the world that claim it is impossible and counter to what God wants.

Representation also carries important theological implications for women in the church. Just as it expands our understanding of

---

12 Ibid.

who can proclaim God's story, it expands our understanding of God and the way we know and reflect that in our own humanity. This is the fullness of the importance of women seeing someone who looks like them at the altar and in the pulpit. When the church reflects the diversity of all of God's people, we come to know the depth of God's love more fully. We come to know that we are included in the messages of grace. These things do not go unnoticed.

When asked what a feminist church looks like, Rev. Amanda Lee replied, "It is where I work now." She went on to explain that her whole staff is women under forty. In reflecting on this she said, "There is a very different office atmosphere that everyone notices when they come in. We are redefining what works for us. For her this means complete flexibility in work structures—helping staff prioritize family life, working from home when needed, and being truly supportive of each other." These women are building the world they want to live in, even if just in a small corner that is their church office.

But for Amanda, the real importance is that people notice the all-female staff. That is the gift of representation to the shared life of the church. In her congregation, people are getting a glimpse of what justice and compassion look like as they embody this call from God. When that happens, they are called to share and build that in all places of this world. This is how we start to recognize the way these realities reflect the fullness of who we are and how we live that out together in this world.

The fullness of life that our God desires for humanity does not end at gender. A feminist church reflects the rich, beautiful diversity of God's people. This means centering marginalized voices and raising up leaders who have long found themselves on the fringes of the church.

I was ordained just a few months after the first female presiding bishop of the ELCA took office. The bishop of my ordaining synod was also a woman. During the service, the two bishops prayed for by name looked like me. But that reality is still held away from many who are queer, transgender, nonbinary, Black, Indigenous, or non-white.

A feminist church will continue to offer us something different than what we have always known and a chance to live into the rich complexity of our human experience. These intersecting identities can become a point of celebration as we recognize all that we are and all that we are called to be together.

Embodiment

A feminist church will be embodied. Just as we live out our lives as enfleshed beings who think and feel, we recognize that our faith is rooted in the incarnation—God coming into our humanity through Christ being born of Mary. In response to the way we profess our understanding of who God is, we live out our faith through our own embodiment. The role of women's bodies and experiences is central to this story of our faith. The church has a particular opportunity to be the place we recognize and celebrate that.

Mary, the mother of Jesus, is the epitome of this understanding. As the *Theotokos*, the "God-bearer," we recognize Mary's role in bringing God's presence into this world through her pregnancy and birthing of Jesus. Despite the adoration of Mary and her role in the incarnation, often the recognized importance of her body ends at Christ's birth. There is little consideration of the care and nurture that mothering encompasses. (This is meant in all ways that mothering love is manifested in this world, not exclusively through biological parenting.)

These acts of motherhood show the role of a woman's body far beyond labor and delivery. These are the very ways in which a woman's body is central to life. It is essential to recognize this when we consider that Jesus came as an infant and not as a grown adult when entering our world. It is here that the embodiment of a woman's experience is most necessary to consider for what it means to have a God who took on our humanity and what it means for women clergy today.

Mary's actions through her body became the way Christ came into this world, was nourished and sustained, was comforted and cherished. Mary's biology enabled her to do what a man could not have accomplished. When we do not appreciate the wide breadth of all that Mary's body did for Jesus, we limit the role of women's bodies in all spaces.

A feminist church must claim this embodied theology, not only in the way we profess our faith but also through our very beings. This means recognizing that all women are called to bring forth ways of knowing God's presence into the world. The creativeness of women is an essential act of God entering our world. Far too often, the church has limited the ability of women to do this because of their gender. In actuality, women have been the ones all along birthing the very presence of God.

Sadly, it is often the embodiment of Jesus as a man that has most stood in the way of women fully living out their calls to serve as ones who would represent the divine. In some denominations it is explained as the gender of the priest needing to reflect the gender of Jesus. But this issue of Jesus as man goes far beyond who can represent him in worship. Questions of the salvific abilities of a male Christ have long been questioned in feminist theology. As Rosemary Radford Ruether once poignantly asked, "Can a male savior save women?"[13]

Yet at the same time in the gospels we witness a Christ who moves against the societal limitations of first-century Roman-occupied Palestine. Jesus listens to women, respects women, and engages women in ways that are deemed questionable at best. In fact, he holds to his relationships with women even in the face of religious officials who scrutinize his behavior. From his conversation with the woman at the well to the Syrophoenician woman to the hemorrhaging woman, Jesus encountered women from all places and treated them as individuals with stories and agency.[14]

For me the woman who most clearly shows this is the one who anoints Jesus days before his crucifixion. Each evangelist gives us this story in their own telling, a rare convergence of the separate gospel narratives.[15] This story represents the importance of the embodied ministry of women and the way in which Jesus' own embodiment stands to support and affirm that ministry.

According to the telling found in Matthew, Mark, and Luke's gospels, she was a stranger. She showed up with the supplies she needed. Despite the presumed cost of the anointment she brought along and the critique of the disciples who witnessed what she was

[13] Rosemary Radford Ruether, *To Change the World: Christology and Cultural Criticism* (Wipf and Stock, 2001), 45.

[14] John 4:7–31, Mark 7:24–29, Mark 5:21–34.

[15] Matthew 26:6–16; Mark 14:3–9, Luke 7:36–50, John 12:1–8.

doing, she held fast to this response to Jesus' mission. While we do not see what called her to this moment, she lived into it with the fullness of herself despite anything unfolding around her. For this woman, anointing Jesus in this way and at that time was important enough for her to bear the cost of the action. Despite the ridicule of her public act, the financial commitment of the purchase of the ointment, and the lack of true recognition for her witness, she was not swayed from what she had set out to do. In fact, it is through that commitment that we see Jesus defend her action and praise her in front of those who think her actions are worthy of criticism. He boldly claims that "wherever the good news is proclaimed in the whole world, what she has done will be told in remembrance of her."[16]

As I continue to hold this text close in my own life and as a pastor, I am struck by the boldness of Jesus' words and the reality that has carried her work and witness through the past two thousand years. After all, Jesus' prediction came true—we are talking about her and what she did. The story of her witness through her unwavering commitment to what she had come to do for Jesus is the core of this story and that which continues to pull us in to know more and to keep remembering her, even if history has long forgotten her name.

While this story might seem simple, we can find a renewed commitment to understanding this story as the place where the witness and ministry of women in the church have an undeniable place. Hers is a story we cannot help but find ourselves in, reflected in her discipleship and faithfulness, dismissed by (male) authorities that claim to know better, and empowered to be who God called her to be by the very one who sets us free from the oppressive constraints of this world. Just as we proclaim a fullness of Christ's humanity in our faith, we live the fullness of our own humanity in our life of faith. That means that we experience our faith in every way through all that it means to be human. This is how we live our lives and how we know our God fully.

When I attended my first Young Clergy Women International conference, I experienced the profound truth of this embodiment in a new way. We gathered on the first night of the conference in a United Methodist church in midtown Atlanta. As the service began, so did

[16] Mark 14:9.

the singing. Entirely female voices filled this historic sanctuary. The presider and preacher were women. All these years later, I find that there is still not an adequate way to fully describe the experience. It was more than moving, and calling it profound does not do justice to that moment. There is something holy in recognizing the fullness of the embodiment of the church in a wholly women-centered, led, and worshiping space. Even if just in this small way, in this relatively fleeting moment, the embodiment of the church was fully female.

A feminist church will represent the full diversity of all gender identities and expressions. These moments capture a glimpse of something that is so counter to the primary narrative of the two thousand years of our Christian witness and remind us of the holiness of who we are. Through those experiences we are emboldened to build a church where all are fully loved and known, where all bodies bring forth God's love into this world and all are able to live as the body of Christ.

This living embodiment is one of the strongest forms of resistance to the powers of patriarchy. By simply being present, visible, and unapologetically the identity that God has made us to bear in this world, we break the narrative hold that patriarchy has and we have the ability to begin anew.

Benediction

Rev. Elizabeth Eaton was elected to serve as the presiding bishop of the ELCA in 2013. She was the first woman to assume this role. In 2025, in preparation for her retirement, her daughter, Beckah Selnak, wrote an article for *Living Lutheran,* the magazine of the ELCA. She reflected on her mother's lifetime of service to the church and, particularly, the twelve years she spent serving as the presiding bishop. She remembered back to her mother's election, commenting that her dad "had to buy more ties—he hadn't packed for history."[17]

As we go forth to do this work for the sake of the world God made, beyond our congregations and communities, may we pack for history.

---

[17] Beckah Selnak, "Ordinary and Extraordinary: A Ministry of 'Holding It All with Grace,'" *Living Lutheran,* July 17, 2025, https://www.livinglutheran.org/2025/07/ordinary-and-extraordinary/.

May we tell truths that break the silence of sexism.

May we have allies who become apostles, running to tell the good news of new life breaking forth.

May we rejoice in the abundance of God that causes our spirits to dance.

May we see the beauty of the divine in ourselves and in our neighbors, reflecting the one who has made us in their image.

May we embody the witness of who we are and what we are becoming together.

And may we be free to know the promises of God, giving thanks for the women who have gone ahead, blessing those who go with us, and becoming the ancestors those who come after us need.

Afterword

Your grandmother's prayers are still protecting you.
—Lalah Delia[1]

In 1947 Anna Tinsman, Alyce Thompson, and Ruth Kuder started teaching Sunday school in their homes. They had recently moved to Upper Providence Township in the southwest suburbs of Philadelphia. The rapidly expanding suburban space was becoming home to young families. Houses were being built where there had previously been only farmland. As with much of the suburbanization of the mid-twentieth century, new churches often accompanied these new communities. Upper Providence would be no different.

With their growing Sunday school showing the potential for a strong congregation, Anna, Alyce, and Ruth wrote to the president of the synod (what we would now call a bishop) and requested a pastor and a mission start in early 1950. By October of that same year, a new worshiping community, Reformation Lutheran Church, began in the Upper Providence Township building, led by a recent seminary graduate, Pastor Robert Anderson. Three years later they broke ground and moved into their new permanent church home.

Those first years were exceptionally formative to the congregation. But during that same time women had no formal leadership. All the official work of the congregation was done by men. Alyce, Anna, and Ruth could not even serve on the congregation's council, let alone serve as a pastor. Despite being the three who were instrumental in starting this church, they had to step aside and let the men in the community take over. They continued teaching Sunday school and supporting the work of the church in every other conceivable, unrecorded way.

Even though I did not have the privilege of meeting them, I know the story of Anna, Alyce, and Ruth well because I now serve as one

[1] Lalah Delia, "Your Grandmother's prayers—are still protecting you," X, September 6, 2016, https://twitter.com/LalahDelia/status/773350553480945665?lang=en.

of the pastors of that congregation. I am grateful for their witness. I am even more grateful that their role has not been forgotten and their names are always the way we start to share our history as a congregation. It has been seventy-five years since the congregation began, and all the clergy at Reformation at this time are women. It is a reality with a significance that is not lost on me.

I share their story as it always reminds me of two questions I seek to live with, especially in the midst of this work: How did we get here? Where do we go from here? These have been my guide from the beginning.

Audacious Hope

This project has shown to be hard and holy work. The stories I heard during the course of this research were heartbreaking. So many times I would finish a conversation with a colleague about her experiences and immediately comment to my husband how awful the church is. Yet, despite this pain and brokenness, I remain full of hope for what still might be. I am hopeful because I love the church. I am hopeful because I see signs of hope.

But what is hope? Hope is often considered to be some ethereal thing, something hard to capture and that in a fleeting moment could drift away altogether. But it is not some delicate thing "with feathers."[2] Rather, it is a tough, unceasing, rugged expression of our humanity. In early 2022 a quote went viral on social media describing hope in a new way: "People speak of hope as if it is this delicate, ephemeral thing made of whispers and spider's webs. It's not. Hope has dirt on her face, blood on her knuckles, the grit of the cobblestones in her hair, and just spat out a tooth as she rises for another go."[3]

To me this is a shared understanding among the women who are refusing to allow patriarchy to continue its reign. There is a camaraderie that can only be fueled by audacious hope of what we catch glimpses of and know is possible. Laura Bates, founder of the Everyday Sexism Project, defines this best. She writes, "It's the power

---

[2] Emily Dickinson, "'Hope' Is the Thing with Feathers," *The Poems of Emily Dickinson,* ed. R. W. Franklin (Harvard University Press, 1999).

[3] Karie Charlton, "Hope Is a Shape-Shifter," *The Presbyterian Outlook,* January 5, 2023, https://pres-outlook.org/2023/01/hope-is-a-shape-shifter/.

of a generation of young women coming to the world and finding it wanting, and a generation of women who've fought this fight already rolling their sleeves back up to return to the fray and finish the job for good. It's the power of a movement that is spreading like an epidemic, that sees injustice in its path and will not be silenced as it has been silenced before."[4]

This is what hope looks like when it gets to work. This is what continues to move us forward despite everything that would try to hold us back. This is the way we answer the call to be the church in the world, lifting up the people of God and celebrating the gifts of women where they have been previously ignored. Hope reminds us of what is possible and invites us to dream with her of all that can be.

It is something that I continue to see in the church. These examples of hope continue to astound and amaze me. Despite the heartbreak of sexism, hope refuses to concede. My own tradition and context have provided me with more glimpses of that than I can count. Here are just a few of those that continue to remind and inspire me to remember the call to this hard and holy work.

For the past several years I have been intently following bishop elections across the ELCA—and for good reason. Things are changing. Each spring I track upcoming elections and watch social media pages for posted results. I do this in synods I have never visited and watch vote tallies for clergy I have never met. While the process of electing a bishop in my denomination has some inherent intrigue, there are significant elections that continue to happen, especially in terms of gender equity.

A bit of history helps to put this into perspective. While women were first granted the ability to be ordained in the Lutheran Church in 1970, it would take until 1992 for the first woman to be elected bishop, when April Larson would assume the position in the La Crosse Area Synod. She remained the only woman, of sixty-five bishops, in the Conference of Bishops for three years. It would take another twenty-six years for the first Black woman to be elected bishop, when Patricia Davenport was elected to serve the Southeastern Pennsylvania Synod

[4] Laura Bates, *Everyday Sexism: The Project that Inspired a Worldwide Movement* (New York: St. Martin's Press, 2016), 378.

in 2018 (a meaningful and historic election that I participated in, as this is my synod and Bishop Davenport was my bishop). The climb for women in these public roles was slow and arduous. But since 2010, the number of women bishops has increased dramatically. Before that year's elections only 9 percent of the ELCA bishops were women. Each year, more and more women have continued to be elected—with some bishop classes being fully female. The 2021 bishop elections would cause the balance to tip for the first time. Now more than 50 percent of the bishops in the ELCA are female.[5] Hope is persistent.

And there are examples of hope in the Lutheran church globally too. I was part of a clergy trip to the Holy Land in January 2023. During our trip we visited the Church of the Redeemer, an English-speaking Lutheran congregation in Old City Jerusalem. While there we met Sally Azar ten days before her ordination. She would be the first woman ordained in the Evangelical Lutheran Church in Jordan and the Holy Land—seventeen years after women were granted the right to be ordained in that denomination.[6] The women clergy on the trip were invited to bless her. We surrounded her, laid hands on her, and sang the doxology. My heart and eyes were filled. It was a long time coming, but hope never loosened its grip. It held tight to a dream of a church that could be yet made real. Sally has come to embody that for so many women and girls throughout Jordan and the Holy Land who have waited to see someone who looks and speaks like them leading a church. Hope is relentless.

The presence and reality of hope continue to fill my days of ministry and surprise me at every turn. Recently I was speaking with a member of my church about another congregation where both clergy are women. In reflecting on how the same is true for our congregation, she asked, "Is that how it is now? Are there more women clergy out there? Or are we just lucky?" She meant this in all sincerity. Having two women serve as her pastors made her feel lucky. And her comment made me know how truly lucky I am. When so

[5] Michael Rinehart, "ELCA Bishops Who Happen to Be Women," *Bishop Michael Rinehart,* updated August 2025, https://bishopmike.com/2020/08/30/elca-bishops-who-happen-to-be-women/.

[6] The ELCJHL voted to allow women's ordination in 2006. This information was provided to me by the Rev. Ashraf Tannous, pastor of Christmas Lutheran Church in Bethlehem, a congregation of the ELCJHL.

many women clergy receive messages opposite of this, I know that I have a rare and beautiful place, a place that I believe is part of Alyce, Anna, and Ruth's dream. Hope is grace-filled.

While these examples are from my tradition and experience, I am confident that these moments of hope cross denominational lines and traditions. Hope is constant and unrelenting—thanks be to God. These signs are what we need to know that a feminist church is possible. Change can happen, and when we champion it the possibilities are more than we can "ask or imagine."[7] Knowing and living this is the greatest act of faith and the greatest act of resistance and hope fills us with strength for all the days ahead. We are called to live in this beautiful, challenging place that hope has brought us to and from which God calls us forward.

[7] Ephesians 3:20.

Acknowledgements

My deepest and greatest thanks are due to so many who have helped to bring this book into the world. First and foremost are the clergywomen who added their voices to this work. Their stories are the hope of what the future rests on.

I am also grateful to all who have been part of shaping me into the person and pastor I am today. Among them are Dr. Karla Bohmbach, who first taught me to love this space where the study of religion and feminism intersect; Dr. Natalia Marandiuc, who oversaw my research throughout my doctoral work; Rev. Dr. Karyn Wiseman, Dr. Jon Pahl, and Deacon Mary Kay DuChene, who served on my defense panel and encouraged me to keep going with this project; Rev. Lynette Chapman, who first showed me what a woman in ministry looks like; Rev. Wayne Matthias-Long, who was a true partner in ministry; Deacon Beth Barkhau and Rev. Eileen Ruppel-Doan, who have given me the privilege of being their colleagues in ministry and for making each day of this work better.

I give thanks for Young Clergy Women International, especially the YCWI Board and Rev. Courtney Smith Westerlund—the outstanding Chalice liaison.

Thank you to Brad Lyons and the whole team at Chalice Press for responding to every question and being the type of ally that all clergywomen need.

Special thanks to the incredible people of God at Reformation Lutheran Church, Media, Pennsylvania, without whom I would not have one of the greatest privileges of my life—being called to serve as a pastor in that place. Your love and encouragement are something I cherish every day.

Last, but never least, thanks to the ones who cheer me on relentlessly—my family. My beloved husband, Dan, my incredible parents, Tish and Jim, and the friend who became family, Julie.

And, of course, to all the cats I have been blessed to have as writing assistants—Pearl, Luna, and Rory.

Ad gloriam maiorem Dei.

Bibliography

Arca, Deborah. "Emergence Christianity: A Whole Lotta Shakin' Goin' On." *Patheos.* January 8, 2013. https://www.patheos.com/blogs/faithforward/2013/01/emergence-christianity-a-whole-lotta-shakin-goin-on/.

Allison, Emily Joy. *#ChurchToo: How Purity Culture Upholds Abuse and How to Find Healing.* Minneapolis: Broadleaf Books, 2021.

Association of Teaching Theologians. "Bishops' Panel." *2021 Association of Teaching Theologians Convocation.* July 26, 2021.

Barna. "Excerpt: A Rapid Decline in Pastoral Security." March 15, 2023. https://www.barna.com/research/pastoral-security-confidence/.

Bates, Laura. *Everyday Sexism: The Project that Inspired a Worldwide Movement.* New York: St. Martin's Press, 2016.

BBC. "Ruth Bader Ginsburg in Pictures and Her Own Words." September 19, 2020. https://www.bbc.com/news/world-us-canada-54218139.

Bolz-Weber, Nadia. "Vox Femina." *The Corners.* March 12, 2023. https://thecorners.substack.com/p/vox-femina#:~:text=May%20young%20girls%20playing%20in,grow%20to%20lead%20us%20all.

Bradner, Eric and Gregory Krieg. "Kamala Harris, as First Woman Elected VP, Says She 'Won't Be the Last," *CNN.* November 7, 2020. https://www.cnn.com/2020/11/07/politics/kamala-harris-speech/index.html.

Brenan, Megan. "Women Still Handle Main Household Tasks in the U.S." *Gallup.* January 29, 2020.https://news.gallup.com/poll/283979/women-handle-main-household-tasks.aspx.

Caldwell, Sophie. "Read the 'Barbie' Monologue that Provoked Such an Emotional Reaction Among Viewers." *Today.* August 2, 2023. https://www.today.com/popculture/movies/america-ferrara-barbie-monologue-full-text-reaction-rcna96237.

CBS News. "More Than 12M 'Me Too' Facebook Posts, Comments, Reactions in 24 Hours." October 17, 2017. https://www.cbsnews.com/news/metoo-more-than-12-million-facebook-posts-comments-reactions-24-hours/.

Center for American Women and Politics. 2025. "History of Women Governors." New Brunswick, NJ: Center for American Women and Politics, Eagleton Institute of Politics, Rutgers University-New Brunswick. https://cawp.rutgers.edu/facts/levels-office/statewide-elective-executive/history-women-governors.

Charlton, Karie. "Hope Is a Shape-Shifter." *The Presbyterian Outlook.* January 5, 2023. https://pres-outlook.org/2023/01/hope-is-a-shape-shifter/.

Chesterton, Eric. "Kiké Hernandez Decided to Stand on a Bucket for His Postgame Interview." *MLB.* April 20, 2017. https://www.mlb.com/cut4/dodgers-kike-hernandez-stood-on-a-bucket-in-his-postgame-interview-c225429262.

Clawson, Julie. "Emergence Christianity, Women, and the Fall of Christendom." *onehandclapping: incantations at the edge of uncertainty.* January 14, 2013. http://julieclawson.com/2013/01/14/emergence-christianity-women-and-the-fall-of-christendom/.

Cooper, Sarah. *How to Be Successful Without Hurting Men's Feelings: Non-Threatening Leadership Strategies for Women.* Kansas City, MO: Andrews McMeel Publishing, 2018.

Cox, Daniel and Kelsey Eyre Hammond. "Young Women Are Leaving Church in Unprecedented Numbers: The Gender Divide in Religiosity has Flipped." *Survey Center on American Life.* April 4, 2024. https://www.americansurveycenter.org/newsletter/young-women-are-leaving-church-in-unprecedented-numbers/.

Daly, Mary. *Beyond God the Father: Toward a Philosophy of Women's Liberation.* Boston: Beacon Press, 1973. Revised 1993.

Davis, Celeste. "Is the Goal of Feminism to Win at Patriarchy?" *Matriarchal Blessing.* June 9, 2024. https://celestemdavis.substack.com/p/goal-of-feminism.

Dickinson, Emily. "'Hope' Is the Thing with Feathers." *The Poems of Emily Dickinson.* Edited by R. W. Franklin. Harvard University, Press, 1999.

Diehl, Amy, Leanne M. Dzubinski, and Amber L. Stephenson. "New Research Reveals the 30 Critiques Holding Women Back from Leadership that Most Men Will Never Hear." *Fast Company.* May 2, 2023. https://www.fastcompany.com/90889985/new-research-reveals-critiques-holding-women-back-from-leadership-that-most-men-will-never-hear.

Disney, Walt, prod. *Cinderella.* Walt Disney Films, 1950.

Episcopal Church, The. "An Episcopal Dictionary of the Church: Ordination of Women." https://www.episcopalchurch.org/glossary/ordination-of-women/.

Evangelical Lutheran Church in America. "ELCA Church Council Votes to Remove 'Vision and Expectations.'" March 8, 2020. https://elca.org/News-and-Events/8027.

Evangelical Lutheran Church in America. "45th Anniversary of the Ordination of Women—Executive Summary Clergy Questionnaire Report 2015." https://download.elca.org/ELCA%20Resource%20Repository/45th_Anniversary_of_the_Ordination_Women_Lay_Full_Report.pdf.

Evangelical Lutheran Church in America. "50th Anniversary Ordination of Women Survey Report." August 2021. Updated March 2022. https://resources.elca.org/gender-justice-and-womens-empowerment/50th-anniversary-ordination-of-women-survey-report-2/.

Felsenthal, Edward. "The Choice: Time's Editor-In-Chief on Why the Silence Breakers Are the Person of the Year." *Time.* https://time.com/time-person-of-the-year-2017-silence-breakers-choice/.

Friedan, Betty. *The Feminine Mystique.* New York: W.W. Norton & Company, 1963.

Gerwig, Greta, dir. *Barbie.* Warner Brothers, 2023.

Graham, Ruth and Elizabeth Dias. "Southern Baptists Vote to Further Expand Restrictions on Women as Leaders." *New York*

Times. June 14, 2023. https://www.nytimes.com/2023/06/14/us/southern-baptist-women-pastors-ouster.html.

hooks, bell. *Feminism Is for Everybody: Passionate Politics.* Cambridge, MA: South End Press, 2000.

hooks, bell. *Feminist Theory: From Margin to Center.* Boston: South End Press, 1984.

Intrabartola, Lisa. "What Mikie Sherrill and Abigail Spanberger's Gubernatorial Wins Mean for Women in Politics. Rutgers. November 5, 2025. https://www.rutgers.edu/news/what-mikie-sherrill-and-abigail-spanbergers-gubernatorial-wins-mean-women-politics.

Knoll, Benjamin R. and Cammie Jo Bolin. "It's Good for Girls to Have Clergywomen, Study Shows." *Religion News.* July 17, 2018. https://religionnews.com/2018/07/17/its-good-for-girls-to-have-clergywomen-study-shows/.

Knoll, Benjamin R. and Cammie Jo Bolin. *She Preached the Word: Women's Ordination in Modern America.* Oxford University Press, 2018.

Lister, Kate. "Women, Would You Rather Be Stuck in a Forest with a Man or a Bear?" *The i Paper.* April 23, 2024. https://inews.co.uk/opinion/women-rather-stuck-forest-with-man-bear-3019615?fbclid=IwY2xjawLkZ5ZleHRuA2FlbQIxMQBicmlkETFOOG4wcGF1TncyOFkwNXJhAR5xEJvNM_aqB40IaqXOzCax-zvaDPm7kIbHVXD4-XlGiGP9-5g2gh0-TLNe8g_aem_85pqie5p4cyUJhGbalfcDg.

Marlow, Toby and Lucy Moss. *Six: The Musical.* December 18, 2017.

Mayo Clinic Staff. "Chronic Stress Puts Your Health at Risk." https://www.mayoclinic.org/healthy-lifestyle/stress-management/in-depth/stress/art-20046037.

McInally, Tom. "Commentary: Why Do United Methodists Ordain Women When the Bible Specifically Prohibits It?" The United Methodist Church. https://www.umc.org/en/content/commentary-mcinally-why-do-united-methodists-ordain-women.

Nevertheless She Preached. https://www.neverthelessshepreached.com/.

North Carolina Synod (ELCA). "'Seriously?' Women in Ministry Video." October 10, 2018. YouTube. https://www.youtube.com/watch?v=bTcaAkG86QQ.

O'Kane, Caitlin. "Maura Healey and Tina Kotek Make History, Winning Elections to Be First

Openly Lesbian U.S. Governors." *CBS News.* November 8, 2022. https://www.cbsnews.com/news/maura-healey-massachusetts-tina-kotek-oregon-elected-governor-first-openly-lesbian-history/.

Paskin, Willa. "Greta Gerwig's 'Barbie' Dream Job." *The New York Times Magazine.* July 17, 2023. https://www.nytimes.com/2023/07/11/magazine/greta-gerwig-barbie.html.

Presbyterian News Services. "PC(USA) Celebrates 60 Years of Women Clergy." PC(USA). May 24, 2016. https://pcusa.org/news-storytelling/news/2016/5/24/pcusa-celebrates-60-years-women-clergy.

Putka, Sophie. "Why Are There No Crash Test Dummies That Represent Average Women?" *Discover Magazine.* February 16, 2021. https://www.discovermagazine.com/technology/why-are-there-no-crash-test-dummies-that-represent-average-women.

Radford Ruether, Rosemary. *To Change the World: Christology and Cultural Criticism.* New York: Crossroad, 1981.

Rinehart, Michael. "ELCA Bishops Who Happen to Be Women." *Bishop Michael Rinehart.* Updated August 2025. https://bishopmike.com/2020/08/30/elca-bishops-who-happen-to-be-women/.

Rogers, Richard and Oscar Hammerstein II. "Impossible." *Cinderella.* 1957. Williamson Music Company (ASCAP), Concord Music Publishing.

Roske-Metcalfe, Andrea. "Do & Don't: An Open Letter to Older Male Senior Pastors Regarding Your Working Relationships with Younger Women/Femme/Non-Binary* Associate Colleagues." *Fidelia Magazine* (Young Clergy Women International). June 5, 2018. https://youngclergywomen.org/do-dont-an-open-letter-to-older-male-senior-pastors-regarding-your-working-relationships-with-younger-women-femme-non-binary-associate-colleagues/?fbclid=IwAR3Df_0Nff8a8JnvlhE3BpoAEmBYiDc52953HFRopE_B_fyMwptqZ7Hhkwg.

Rothaus, Kyndall Rae. *Thy Queendom Come: Breaking Free from the Patriarchy to Save Your Soul.* Minneapolis: Broadleaf Books, 2021.

Ruether, Rosemary. *To Change the World: Christology and Cultural Criticism.* Wipf and Stock, 2001.

Sanders, Bo. "Preferring the Past: Phyllis Tickle, Radical Orthodoxy and the Tea Party." *Tripp Fuller.* January 18, 2013. https://trippfuller.com/2013/01/18/preferring-the-past-phyllis-tickle-radical-orthodoxy-and-the-tea-party/.

Selnak, Beckah. "Ordinary and Extraordinary: A Ministry of 'Holding It All with Grace.'" *Living Lutheran.* July 17, 2025. https://www.livinglutheran.org/2025/07/ordinary-and-extraordinary/.

Smith, Morgan. "'It's a Disastrous Situation': Women Leaders Are Leaving Companies at the Highest Rate Ever." *CNBC.* October 18, 2022. https://www.cnbc.com/2022/10/18/women-leaders-are-leaving-companies-at-highest-rate-ever-leanin-mckinsey-co-report.html.

Steber, Eleanor. "One Little Leap at a Time." *Western Canadian Moravian Historical Magazine* 18 (April 2013). Canadian Moravian Historical Society. https://www.moravian.org/wp-content/uploads/sites/7/2018/10/Moravian_Historical_Magazine-No_18.pdf.

Steinem, Gloria. "News." *Gloria Steinem.* http://www.gloriasteinem.com/news#:~:text=%22Without%20leaps%20of%20imagination%2C%20or,is%20a%20form%20of%20planning.%22.

Stephens-Reed, Laura. "Ways Male Senior Pastors Can Be Great Allies for Their Clergywomen Colleagues." *Laura Stephens-Reed.* April 25, 2023. https://www.laurastephensreed.com/blog/ways-male-senior-pastors-can-be-great-allies-for-their-clergywomen-colleagues?fbclid=IwAR1YJ4Dm_8ecPJrULVwT9IY6QBUxVMI9rbA_LLjvgdHfRkAi45kFY_4N_zU.

Summers, Chelsea G. "The Politics of Pockets." *Vox.* September 19, 2016. https://www.vox.com/2016/9/19/12865560/politics-of-pockets-suffragettes-women.

Tallon, Tina. "A Century of 'Shrill': How Bias in Technology Has Hurt Women's Voices." *The New Yorker.* September 3, 2019. https://www.newyorker.com/culture/cultural-comment/a-century-of-shrill-how-bias-in-technology-has-hurt-womens-voices.

theSkimm Staff. "The State of Women…Isn't Working." *theSkimm.* March 9, 2023. https://www.theskimm.com/stateofwomen/harris-poll-data-2023.

Tsirkin, Julie and Emma Dion. "Federal Government to Require Car Companies to Use Female Test Dummies." *NBC News.* November 20, 2025. https://www.nbcnews.com/politics/politics-news/dot-female-crash-test-dummy-regulation-rcna244949.

Walker, Alice. *In Search of Our Mother's Gardens.* New York City: Open Road Media, 1983.

Wardell, Amber. "Why Women Say They'd Choose the Bear: A Non-Comprehensive List." *Medium.* May 2, 2024. https://medium.com/@amber_wardell/why-women-say-theyd-choose-the-bear-a-non-comprehensive-list-b35b2e0d60bb.

Wible, Shayna Jo. "Support for Women Who Pastor." *Fidelia Magazine* (Young Clergy Women International). June 16, 2023. https://youngclergywomen.org/support-for-women-who-pastor/.

Women's Transformation and Leadership. "A History of Women in the RCA." Reformed Church in America. https://www.rca.org/equipping-congregations/womens-transformation-leadership/history/#:~:text=Triennial%20gathered%20women%20for%20meaningful,Van%20Es%2C%20and%20Judy%20Nelson.

World Economic Forum. "Global Gender Gap Report 2023." June 20, 2023. https://www.weforum.org/reports/global-gender-gap-report-2023/in-full/benchmarking-gender-gaps-2023/#:~:text=The%20Global%20Gender%20Gap%20score,compared%20to%20last%20year's%20edition.

Young Clergy Women International. "About Us." https://youngclergywomen.org/about/.

www.ingramcontent.com/pod-product-compliance
Lightning Source LLC
Jackson TN
JSHW081906270226
98501JS00006B/20

9780827203532